White-collar unionism:
The rebellious salariat

Clive Jenkins and Barrie Sherman

Routledge & Kegan Paul
London, Boston and Henley

First published in 1979
by Routledge & Kegan Paul Ltd
39 Store Street,
London WC1E 7DD,
Broadway House,
Newtown Road,
Henley-on-Thames,
Oxon RG9 1EN and
9 Park Street,
Boston, Mass. 02108, USA
Set in Journal Roman
and printed in Great Britain by
Lowe & Brydone Printers Ltd
Thetford, Norfolk

British Library Cataloguing in Publication Data

Jenkins, Clive
White-collar unionism.
1. Trade-unions – White collar workers – Great Britain
I. Title   II. Sherman, Barrie
331.88'11   HD6668.M4   79–40213

ISBN 0 7100 0216 5
ISBN 0 7100 0237 8 Pbk

Contents

	Abbreviations	vii
	Introduction	1
1	Who are the white-collar workers?	12
2	The rise and short history of white-collar unionism	23
3	Organisation and recruitment problems of white-collar unions	41
4	The mechanisms of a white-collar union	58
5	Significant gains, significant disputes, significant techniques	71
6	The rewards system	86
7	New legislation	95
8	Incomes policies	112
9	The widening of traditional horizons	124
10	The impact of the white-collar union on Britain	136
11	Managers	140
12	The quality of life	151
13	The future	163
	Index	169

White-collar unionism:
The rebellious salariat

Abbreviations

ACAS	Advisory, Conciliation and Arbitration Service
ACTSS	Association of Clerical, Technical and Supervisory Staffs
AEI	Amalgamated Electrical Industries
AESD	Association of Engineering and Shipbuilding Draughtsmen
APEX	Association of Professional, Executive, Clerical and Computer Staffs
APST	Association of Professional Scientists and Technologists
ASSET	Association of Supervisory Staffs, Executives and Technicians
ASTMS	Association of Scientific, Technical and Managerial Staffs
AUEW	Amalgamated Union of Engineering Workers
BDA	British Dental Association
BIM	British Institute of Management
BLMC	British Leyland Motor Corporation
BMA	British Medical Association
CAC	Central Arbitration Committee
CAWU	Clerical and Administrative Workers' Union
CBI	Confederation of British Industry
CEI	Council of Engineering Institutions
CFDT	Confédération française des travailleurs chrétiens
CGT	Confédération général du travail
CIR	Commission on Industrial Relations
COHSE	Confederation of Health Service Employees
CPSA	Civil and Public Services Association
DATA	Draughtsmen and Allied Technicians' Association
DHSS	Department of Health and Social Security
DoE	Department of Employment

EEF	Engineering Employers' Federation
EEPTU	Electrical, Electronic, Telecommunication and Plumbing Union
EMA	Engineers' and Managers' Association
EPEA	Electrical Power Engineers' Association
FO	Force ouvrière
GEC	General Electric Company
✔ IPCS	Institution of Professional Civil Servants
IRSF	Inland Revenue Staff Federation
✔ MATSA	Managerial Administrative Technical and Supervisory Association
MPU	Medical Practitioners' Union
NALGO	National and Local Government Officers' Association
NAS	National Association of Schoolmasters
NEDC	National Economic Development Council
NEDO	National Economic Development Office
NFA	National Foremen's Association
NFPW	National Federation of Professional Workers
NHS	National Health Service
NIESR	National Institute of Economic and Social Research
NUBE	National Union of Bank Employees
NUET	National Union of Elementary Teachers
NUGMW	National Union of General and Municipal Workers
NUIW	National Union of Insurance Workers
NUM	National Union of Mineworkers
NUPE	National Union of Public Employees
NUR	National Union of Railwaymen
NUS	National Union of Students
NUT	National Union of Teachers
PIB	Prices and Incomes Board
POEU	Post Office Engineering Union
POMSA	Post Office Management Staffs Association
SCS	Society of Civil Servants
SLADE	Society of Lithographic Artists, Designers, Engineers and Process Workers
T&GWU	Transport and General Workers' Union

TASS	Technical, Administrative and Supervisory Section of the Amalgamated Union of Engineering Workers
TSSA	Transport and Salaried Staffs Association
TUC	Trades Union Congress
UCATT	Union of Construction, Allied Trades and Technicians
UIS	Union of Insurance Staffs
UKAPE	United Kingdom Association of Professional Engineers
UNESCO	United Nations Education, Scientific and Cultural Organisation
WVS	Women's Volunteer Service

Introduction

'What is virtue but the Trade Unionism of the married?' – Shaw

The decade of the 1970s saw a remarkable growth in both the size and the influence of the trade-union movement. It now has nearly thirteen-million members* and is the largest and most representative voluntary and democratic movement in the UK, if not the world. It has changed and is changing from the moribund 'cart-horse' image of 'Low' to a more dynamic and thoughtful movement. It is changing because the TUC now has within it almost every strand and tendency of legitimate trade-unionism to a point where those standing outside seem anxious to exemplify the definition of eccentricity. The TUC is now a body of solid and central importance and, as such, it is consulted by governments both national and supranational. In such circumstances no body can rely on being short-term and reactive in outlook and the change to medium-term and pre-emptive policies and argument has been very marked.

It can be argued, and indeed we shall argue, that these changes arise in great part from the wider membership that the movement now encompasses. This has come from a combination of recruitment into the smaller, long-affiliated unions by new affiliations from public sector unions and the major extensions into organisation of the salariat.

In almost all cases these new entrants have been *white-collar workers – the managers of the last quarter of this century.* This recruitment into the trade union mainstream in whatever form it has come, has been compelled by an irresistible political and social logic. But it is a logic which has been misunderstood and underexplained.

The media portrayal of the salaried professional and 'middle' classes operating an organised approach *in concert* with the old established unions has been misleading. The professional observers took the mistaken view that these newcomers were the 'moderates' and somehow

* Certification Officer's Report.

1

favoured a stabilised (or temporarily immobilised) union movement which would sustain an ideal balance of forces in the British mixed economy.

The contrary may well be the case. These newcomers are the dissatisfied groups carrying the scars of six post-war governmental incomes policies and questioning the *status quo*. They additionally may excite the interest of manual workers' unions who note they are arguing from a higher plateau of occupational pensions, longer holidays, shorter working hours and superior sick-pay arrangements. This is becoming a volatile mix; the reagent and catalyst together being the 'new unionism' and the reaction bringing forth a more self-confident and influential national movement. At the same time the so-called 'staff' workers are now found working shifts in computer complexes or in large groups tending office machines in high-rise buildings. The nature of work in the white-collar sector is changing under the pervasive and persuasive impact of technology. This is breaking down the skills previously exclusive to individuals, in the same way as the craftsman lost total control of his output when the subdivision of skills grew and the assembly line came into existence.

Our analysis is that the white-collar worker has become collectivised at work and it follows that he, or she, is now naturally being organised for collective bargaining, but that the impact of this upon the unions, social democracy, parliamentary activity and our society has only recently been conceptualised. It has not yet had a significant effect but it obviously will be of the greatest importance and not in the long run; rather the effect will be felt sooner than later.

This change is taking place against the backcloth of a Britain, indeed the whole world, changing technologically and sociologically at a head-long rate. The rate of change has accelerated through the century especially on the technical side but with leaps arising from world wars; once a product had a twenty-year life, now innovations can reduce it to obsolescence in less than two years. The motor vehicle opened up new horizons to the working family; new building techniques opened the door to adequate housing for many; the computer has been developed to bring a new range of products into the orbit of the employee class; new drugs have extended life expectancy, and television has brought easily-absorbed information into the home.

These changes have created uncertainties where certainties (however unpalatable) previously reigned; created mobility where stratification prevailed and created relative affluence where poverty was endemic. Social change has not kept pace with the technological changes and the resulting state of flux has stimulated both the decline of institutions which were taken for granted and the rise of new authorities, and changed the relative importance of these institutions in everyday life. Religion has declined, the power of the Press has been questioned, television has become influential and the cashless society is being created, whilst trade unions have expanded in size and in political leverage. The changes in Britain have changed the emphasis to the present and the immediate future rather than the longer term, probably because all these uncertainties have made life that much more complex and difficult for those who must enter the labour market.

It is, of course, not only the pace of the change – it is the type of change that is important too. Both local and central government have been increasingly impinging on people's lives and although this may be civilising it has brought with it bureaucracy and a legal jargon, which mystify rather than enlighten. National legislation now directly affects everyday aspects of life as it becomes more pervasive, affecting shopping, house purchase or rental, health and industrial relations. Both at home and at the workplace the simple tasks taken for granted just two decades ago have become complex administrative instruments with contractual obligations, statutory duties and constraints. In this society advisory specialists became essential to cut through the jargon and to protect and advise those who lack either the time, the expertise, or the inclination, to protect themselves. This means that the solicitor or the accountant can attract premiums for services to a point where they are inaccessible to the majority of people. For the salaried worker who may detect his vulnerability sooner a trade union can now fill the need and bridge the gap.

The trade union has thus become an essential part of the social defence and meets representational needs. This is especially true when doomed incomes policies trundle after each other and spectacular new laws such as the Industrial Relations Act, 1971, the Employment Protection Act and the Industry Act are enacted. When equal pay, equal opportunities, pensions and health and safety measures also require both decisions and quasi-legal expertise, the need for professional aid becomes more manifest to even the most apathetic of employees. The challenge and the responsibilities of proposed industrial democracy legislation is making union membership an imperative.

The original concept of a trade union was simple enough in a crude power-relations dominated society. The individual worker could not stand up to an individual employer in any confrontation situation. The employer with the right to hire and fire had the balance of advantages on his side. The idea that workers collectively might be stronger and could counter this imbalance was the motivating force behind the trade union movement's creation. This underpinning remains today as the most important single premise; collective action is the key and it is this fundamental that the drafters of the Industrial Relations Act, 1971 either did not comprehend or ignored and explains why so much hostility was directed at it. It was unknowing legislation.

At the time when the trade unions were struggling to overcome not only employer hostility but linked government and establishment obstructionism, the main concern was to seek a living wage (in the strict construction), to fight wage cuts and to shorten the working week. At a slightly later date, working conditions and the exploitation of child and female labour became central issues. There was no subtlety, nor were conditions then conducive to anything other than basic struggles – it was a matter of life and death rather than living standards, differentials, job evaluation or joint management of the labour force.

The structure of the trade unions tended to match the structure of the emerging industries: textiles, coal, iron and steel, shipbuilding, railways and heavy engineering. A lack of mobility following the initial move from agriculture to the towns often meant that unions were locally or company based. The difficulty in communications meant that federations were difficult to set up and, when organised, difficult to service and maintain. The craftsmen were the only unionised people at this time, unskilled workers were slow to create unions while white-collar or staff unionism was not envisaged. There was no large public or service sector employing essentially non-manual workers. Managers in the production industries were still few and far between; it was the age of the entrepreneur not of the corporate monolith. The transnational corporation did not yet exist as we know it today, although its ancestors, trading companies such as the East Indian Company, were starting to work.

Whilst the original concept remains, society has changed and so have trade unions and their functions. Increased mobility and access to information have made most of them nationally based; the changes in the structure of employment have meant that craft-based unions have declined whilst general and white-collar unions have expanded. The growth of government direction of the economy and industry has meant that more and more employees need competent representation to cope with factors which are complex, time-consuming and at least one remove from the workplace; such problems demand professional expertise for their successful resolution.

There are now nearly 12 million members of TUC-affiliated trade unions out of an employed workforce of 23 million and a population of 56 million. This union penetration figure, as high as it is at over 50 per cent, actively understates the unions' success. There are 1·9 million self-employed in the labour force, and 600,000 in other bodies such as the police and the armed forces, neither of which are at present eligible for trade union membership. There are many workers in the agriculture, distribution and construction industries who are part-time or casual employees and thus unlikely to join trade unions. The penetration figure is thus, in reality, well over 60 per cent. In contractual negotiations the trade unions bargain on behalf of 16 million employees, the other 5 million being in bargaining areas but not union members. To many trade unionists the behaviour of some of these 5 million, especially the minority who are vocally critical of trade unions, is reprehensible but this non-union group in manufacturing and commerce is steadily being eroded. When compared with the membership of the Labour and Conservative Parties, and nationally based voluntary organisations such as (say) the WVS, the trade union movement in numbers alone dwarfs the rest.

It is now a base for new ideas. As the largest of possible organised democratic pressure groups it contains disparate organisations and rarely speaks with a single voice although policy decisions are made on a majority vote at the annual TUC and on the General Council in between times. These decisions are influential despite any arguments which may precede them.

There are private-sector and public-sector unions; mixed private- and public-sector unions; some are white-collar, some larger unions have white-collar sections; some are based on a trade or craft; others have a more general membership. In some, women are in the majority, in others there are no women at all. The range extends from the very low-paid to the relatively well-remunerated salaried classes and embraces all industries and services. The disparity means that there must be conflicting interests within the TUC at any one time as in society generally. These conflicts are resolved by discussion and by compromise as they are in other bodies.

The changes that have taken place in society are mirrored in the trade unions themselves. As industry becomes more dominated by amalgamations and the number of leading companies dwindle through a process of take-overs and the birth of conglomerates, so the number of trade unions has fallen. In 1951 there were 186 unions, in 1955 there were 183, and in 1977 there were 115 affiliated to the TUC. This diminution of 37 per cent over 26 years has been matched by an increase in total membership of TUC-affiliated unions, over the same period, from 7·83 million to 11·51 million; an increase of 47 per cent. This feature of more members in fewer unions is comparable to the trend in commerce and industry to fewer enterprises with higher total turnover and profits. The average membership of a trade union has risen from nearly 43,000 to over 100,000 in this period and is testimony to this powerful trend to concentration and enlargement.

This is a macroscopic view. Later in the book we examine the decline and growth of different unions in different sectors, trades and on status basis. It shows, contrary to unknowing opinion, that the trade union movement is not static and may even be more dynamic than any other social sector. The parallel in industry is that the top 100 firms increased their proportion of output from 24 per cent in 1935 to 43 per cent in 1970 and it is now estimated that it has reached 50 per cent. This dynamic is reflected in other ways. The basic demands made by trade union members of their unions have changed from those of negotiation on basic minima to a more sophisticated package of 'total remuneration'.

Joint settlement of job security, environmental concern and participation in management decisions are now all firmly within the sights of trade unionists. This places more strain on a trade union in that expertise has to be gained in subjects which hitherto have been neglected due to a lack of demand. It has unfortunately had the consequence of making the traditional bargaining skills of many officials redundant, resembling the trauma of craftsmen in a numerically controlled machine age. Not all unions have responded to the new pressures and not all members have exerted a pressure but the trend again is unmistakable and powerful. In some senses it is unfortunate that the white-collar union sector seems to be taking the lead in this matter – because of the friction and misunderstandings that may be created as they are associated with an elitist image.

Trade unions are primarily concerned with the welfare of their employed members and with the families of their members. However, in an increasingly inter-related and complex world the old routine of a yearly in-plant negotiation is totally inappropriate. The growth of the conglomerate and vertical integration in industry has meant that the secondary effects of either management or union actions are more quickly felt and have wider and deeper repercussions within a national economy. An example of this is the effect that a slow-down in the car industry has on all the supplier firms in glass, tyres or plastics. This change has resulted in greater care in the selection of industrial dispute tactics because action taken to improve the welfare of one group of workers may involve sacrifices by groups of non-involved workers; more contact is now made between the parties and more thought is given to the consequences but this is still at a primitive level.

This growth of the large unit has stimulated some growth in trade-union membership and especially in the white-collar private sector. The large enterprise is impersonal and imparts to employees a sense of insecurity rather than stability. Decisions affecting job security, job content and salaries are taken by executives far removed from line management and, very often, removed geographically. One can consider a conglomerate where decisions are most often taken by managers with little or no knowledge of the single firm, or foreign-owned multi-nationals where the decisions are taken on another continent.

For white-collar staffs this is a most important development. They have not, in relation to manual workers, been particularly well paid in the past, despite common and widely held beliefs to the contrary. Employees on 'staff' (the Bob Cratchits of this world) were compensated by shorter working hours, better working conditions, higher social status, in-work familiarity with senior management or owners and, most importantly, greater job security. In many instances the move towards a 'single status' has removed the non-wage remuneration advantages; social status is declining at the same rate as inverse money differentials advance, and the large organisation has removed the personal touch. The white-collar employee now feels deprived of the traditional advantages and is well aware of the newer disadvantages; these, together, now lead to trade union membership. The large enterprise also has the effect of stimulating equally large countervailing groups merely as a result of the size of the enterprise with a minimum of philosophical underpinning. But white-collar trade unionism is not the exciting new phenomenon often presented by newspapers and academics who have stumbled across its latest manifestations. The NUT, the various Civil Service unions, the police organisations and the national and local government officers have all been in the field for most of this century with substantial memberships. The private-sector bodies developed later although important embryonic organisations have existed as a result of the stimulation of the First World War. But their membership has accelerated markedly since the Second World War as governments have nationalised, denationalised and tinkered with overall control of the economy and particularly, starting with the interventions of Sir Stafford Cripps in 1948, in the sensitive area of incomes policy.

One reason why there is an apparently huge growth is that unions are often defined as organisations affiliated to the TUC. This is fair and realistic but a number of legitimate white-collar unions used to exist outside the TUC and have joined only recently, for example, NALGO, SCS and the IPCS. This has caused an exaggerated media reaction. In addition there are many quasi- or pseudo-unions which registered as trade unions under the provisions of the 1971 Industrial Relations Act. It can properly be argued that TUC membership is, *per se*, the only true definition of a trade union but in the 'white-collar' context there have been historic problems surrounding this move to affiliation. These however are rapidly being overcome. The act of becoming a member of a union where there is no previous history or ethos of unionisation used to be a brave one – even in the 1960s – whether or not that organisation was TUC affiliated. It is the act of joining that is significant. There are, however, situations where such an act is not at all significant because not only is there no employer hostility but employer encouragement as an act of manipulation. This is the case where a staff association is formed (in reaction to a bona fide trade union attempt to organise in the area) with management providing cash subsidies, secretarial facilities and accommodation or, in 'sensitive' cases, a concealed subsidy.

Although such staff associations start as creations of management they often now develop a sense of inadequacy and merge with a trade union as the members realise that a representation of their real interests can never take place when they are members of a client or captive organisation.

Britain is a complex, post-imperialist industrial society and, in common with other such societies where there has also been a withdrawal from an empire, has multiple economic, political and sociological difficulties. The trade union movement as a whole (and through the separate unions) makes representations on all of these resultant problems, as do the employers through employers' federations and individual enterprises although, most critically, when in difficulty. This movement of both sides of industry into general policy lobbying is inevitable and will undoubtedly increase over time. It is the badge of a collectivised society. The management of Britain is such that any one action tends to have repercussions on totally remote institutions and bodies as the argument works through the linkages in the economy and in society. For example, a decision to increase the price of school meals has effects on the disposable incomes of parents and this is then translated into either wage demands or demands for extra overtime. It has an effect on teachers' unions, on the demand for school meals and therefore employment in that area and in food and equipment supplying areas; an effect on nutrition and health and thus an impact on total health services, and finally, a sociologically divisive impact. Some of these may be no more than marginal, but the fact that the problems exist will mean that some influential organisations will make representations. Generally speaking, the CBI would be as much in favour of cuts in public expenditure generally as the TUC would see such moves as socially retrogressive. The school teachers' unions, canteen workers' unions, NHS unions and social workers' organisations, as well as food and equipment supplying companies and their unions, will all have an interest and will insist on a voice – preferably before the decision is made.

The role that unions now play has been criticised by some who are apprehensive of trade unions visibly moving into the political arena and do not see the *nature* of the movement. Strangely, such commentators see nothing curious when a company or an employer's organisation makes a similar move. On the union side, whether the activity is at a national level through NEDO, or through individual unions lobbying government departments (sometimes alongside employers), or other agencies, their initial objective is always the protection of a membership. Not only is this an admirable behavioural pattern but a trade union which failed to explore all avenues on behalf of its members' interests would be receiving their subscriptions under false pretences. Members of trade unions take an active decision to transfer part of their income to their unions (tiny though that may be) and, not unnaturally, expect a return for this expenditure. They may even expect a greater return for this expenditure than any other part of their personal budgeting. This may merely be the protection that the union can give simply by existing as a vigorous agent, or an organisation with a reputation, or it can be the type of quasi-political activity referred to above. What is important, especially amongst those who do not have a background in collective bargaining, is that programmes are conceived on their behalf, are seen to be carried on and most importantly get realised.

The new white-collar trade union member tends to exhibit the traditional traits of this special grouping. He or she is articulate, gets information from newspapers rather than television, and is personally ambitious and ambitious for his or her children. This combination can put a strain on the head office and professional negotiating staff of the union since results are expected more quickly than is usual in a non-white-collar union. This has resulted in such unions, who have exhibited fastest growth (ASTMS is a good example), needing to pioneer new bargaining techniques, new uses of the legal system and new lobbying tactics. There is the reverse side of the coin: because the membership has these characteristics, the help given by members is of a high standard and the ideas and information channelled upwards from the membership to negotiators is sophisticated and, providing the professional staff are capable of dealing with it, gives style and quality to presentation.

The pattern of employment within Britain has changed greatly since 1945. There has been a steady drift of employment away from both the traditional infra-structural industries and the manufacturing sector to the public and private service sectors. Superimposed on this movement have been the technological changes due to such developments as computerised production techniques which have released labour on to a market which transformed them into service employees. Ultimately no society can prosper in this way. San Marino may be able to exist on the sale of postage stamps but for a large industrialised economy such as Britain's the trend is very dangerous economically unless the capital intensity gives a greater unit output and creates a greater surplus or profit than older techniques. This in turn helps to explain the growth of white-collar trades unions. High salaries are not available because in general the economy cannot support them and the secure base is not there for a guarantee of continuous employment. A white-collar worker is thus no more than marginally more secure; indeed, we will argue later that he is now perhaps *less* secure than his blue-collar colleagues.

The growth in numbers of white-collar workers has not been due totally to inter-sectorial movements of employees. Technological changes have created far more technical jobs and far more sophisticated service engineering jobs to the extent that some new plants employ mainly white-collar workers. In addition to this change there has been a managerial revolution. The more complex a company's operations or the larger the administrative unit, the more managers are needed. The resulting explosion in demand can be seen reflected in the mushrooming of business schools and colleges, often of vastly different standards of qualification. Managers would not generally describe themselves as white collar: they see themselves as superior and society in general would agree. Despite this perception, or status problem, it is now generally accepted that a whole new class of employees has arisen – the white-collar manual workers.

What defines a white-collar worker? Each definition raises further anomalies and exceptions. For example, is a shop assistant white-collar or is he or she merely in blue-collar employment in an environment which generally does not soil collars at all? This is a futile exercise in semantics and this book will have no truck with this particular game. Many qualified bodies such as UNESCO have tied themselves in knots year after year trying to define a scientist but without success; they have now realised that it is not important and they produce documents which embrace both technologists and scientists. To try to define 'white-collar' precisely is both a restrictive and sterile exercise which will create as many problems as it solves, for technology has long since mocked and discarded such distinctions. Self-perception has not helped union membership drives for we live in a status-ridden society and in the past a personal white-collar classification trailed behind it a tail of anti-union prejudice. In this book, we shall deal with the middle classes, by and large, as employees who have some responsibility or qualification, who expect that the time that they invested in themselves to obtain their qualification or skills will be rewarded and who believe that responsibility – like danger in other people's work – should be reflected in their remuneration. We propose to ignore the tyranny of the job title or job description in discussing the problems of the salariat.

There is nothing startling in the growth of middle-class trade unionism, nor should it be marvelled at. It was historically inevitable and the only issue has been the time scale of its accomplishment. In almost all sectors of economic life in Britain, such employees are moving into a position of numerical superiority but seem still to be at the mercy of employers and their power. In manufacturing, distribution, services and the public sector, white-collar and managerial employees have seen their money differentials over less-skilled employees disappear, often as a result of government incomes policies and sometimes as a result of market forces which they were in no position to influence. When added on to the new job insecurities which resulted from the 1971 recession and the 1975/8 slump, it is remarkable that so few have actually joined the trade union movement. The insurance industry recently advertised by using a slogan, 'Get the strength of the insurance companies around you.' In this modern capitalist world it has been remiss of the white-collar worker not to take that advice in industrial terms and join a trade union. That fault of choice is clearly being reversed but, unfortunately for us all, in conditions of trauma.

Chapter 1

Who are the white-collar workers?

'And there, scarce less illustrious, goes the clerk!' – Cowper

Our attitude is one of detestation for the semantic game of attempting to define a white-collar worker but, as so many find this bristling with difficulties, it may be illuminating to examine just why it *is* so difficult. The term itself is overtly male chauvinistic: women rarely wear white collars, and many dresses, sweaters and blouses have no collars whatsoever. The white-collar terminology arose from the notion that certain employees worked in an environment which was so clean that the white collar could easily be worn without the fear of it being soiled or ruined, whilst for the majority of employees in a dirty environment, this was treated as a natural condition. At this time the work force contained fewer married women. Even in this period there were problems of definition, difficulties which arose out of legal actions and the exceptions and contradictions were in evidence in the late nineteenth century. Since then, organisational structures have become more complex, job titles have become more numerous, technological advances have created blurred technician-based work groups, and government, both local and central, has expanded the number of people employed on clerical and administrative tasks.

Apart from the fact that white collar obviously stems from the days of sartorial elegance (or conservatism whichever way one cares to view it) the concept itself has to a large extent also been displaced. More and more the production line has become automated, factories are dust-free, while machines are self-lubricating and sometimes self-operating; white collars might still be fit to grace a soap powder advertisement after a day in such an environment.

The search for a proper definition has exercised analysts in Britain and elsewhere for many years, to the extent that it has almost become the search for the industrial relations philosopher's stone. Many definitions, some more complex than others, have been offered, but none as yet has managed to overcome the attendant exceptions and anomalies

12

thrown up by the definition itself. Other attempts have, in their own way, merely substituted one value judgment for another. The basic trouble is obvious: it is a status concept, very much in the eye of the person concerned, not the beholder, leading to sociological ramblings and omissions. To add to the confusion, some jobs seem to fall into a permanent grey area and defy attempts at basic or simple classification. Policemen, the armed forces and musicians are examples of groups of workers whose status is indeterminate.

At one time there were radical differences between those who were 'on staff' and those who were 'workers'. Workers clocked-in, staff had, at worst, an honour-book system; workers were on hourly or weekly rates of pay, staff were on weekly or monthly rates; workers had short holiday entitlements, staff had longer leave periods; workers had no sick pay or pension schemes, staff had both; workers could be fired at an hour's notice, staff had a month's notice; and so on. These differences which were once so important in status and job-security terms have become blurred, and in some cases have disappeared altogether as the move towards a single status starts to gather momentum and legislation increasingly modifies terms of employment in a generalised way. There are still major differences and also differing approaches to employment groups by unions, but these of themselves offer little help in definition.

One major definition we found to be quite inadequate early on in our examination divided jobs between those who used their brains and those who used physical strength. This distinction, tenuous at the outset, is rendered almost meaningless by changes in work methods and production techniques and the advent of computerisation. In any event, most jobs require a combination of brain and muscle power and far too many, other than the limited categories of philosophers and tube tunnellers, are too difficult to classify. A second method attempted was the 'functional job content' approach. This involves listing certain functions such as administrative, design, analysis and planning, supervisory, managerial and commercial, with sub-functions within each function. The rationale behind this system is that these were the functions at one time performed by the entrepreneur and that as the size of the concern grew so responsibilities were delegated. Apart from the irrelevance of the delegation argument and the growth of public-sector and non-industrial commercial or other productive sectors, the major defect is again contained in the nomination of the functions and sub-functions themselves and the grey areas so formed. A third method, the so-called eclectic method, is based on whether the employee works in a mechanical or bureaucratic environment, but has to define which is which in a laboratory, or what, say, to do with the site managers in the building industry – the solution to these problems is not stated. A final method of classification is proximity to authority. This argues that the man or woman sitting behind a desk has authority imparted by that desk, but then so does an articulated lorry driver looking down from a lofty driving cabin – so far as the physically lower family car driver is concerned.

The problem is, for all normal working purposes, largely a manufactured irrelevancy. It is important in the context of government or census statistics, but from the point of view of those who are actually doing the work, or the employer and trade unions, there is nothing to be gained. However, from the standpoint of persons writing a book on white-collar unions it is a subject that has to be broached, if only because such unions are, by definition, made up of white-collar workers – or at the least mainly of white-collar workers – because some have a blue-collar support base. In essence, the problem is similar to defining a colour. We name colours and the nuances of shade and tint, yet the colour seen by one individual is by no means the colour seen by another and neither would it be described as such.

The 1971 Census totally begged the question and did not define either white-collar or non-manual, but the New Earnings Survey maintains a list of non-manual occupations and this is used when preparing the Survey itself which sub-divides manual and non-manual employees for analytical purposes. This list maintains eighteen main groups of which nine are non-manual and nine are manual. Within the former nine there are 133 sub-groups and these are themselves sub-divided into over 500 very broad sub-titles.

There are odd discrepancies, for example, computer programmers and office-machine operators are included, but computer operators are not; nurses are, whilst dental auxiliaries are not. Nevertheless, it does represent a reasonable cross-section of jobs *titles*. More to the point it is a list which most people would agree represents white-collar employment, although some of the sub-groups would be controversial if submitted to a public debate, for example, traffic wardens, prison officers or firemen. For the purposes of this analysis such conflict is not important, although public perception *is*. This is certainly not an approach that would pass academic scrutiny because there is no common factor linking the job titles other than a common acceptance that they represent white-collar employment.

In functional terms this is all that is needed. Most people do not consciously think in this idiom although equally most people hold some idea of a ranking order of jobs in their heads and one factor involved in the ranking is whether the job is manual or non-manual. Unfortunately, not too many people agree about the rankings, one major stumbling block being ignorance of the duties involved in certain jobs or indeed what the job title actually means. It will cover the clearly observed distinctions between a refuse collector, a doctor, a stockbroker or a waitress, but large undefined areas remain. One of the reasons for this large gap is that perceptions are based not on objective criteria but on a vaguely prejudiced approach formed from their own experiences and from whatever information sources they usually tap. Most people do not find it necessary to go further than this. Ranking order only becomes important when comparing one salary level against another and the concept of a national salary or job evaluation is not one which has gained any significant degree of acceptance within Britain.

It is relatively rare for employees to think of, or talk of, their jobs in terms of manual or non-manual employment, let alone argue into which category their particular job fits. It is equally rare for a trade union to enter into this debate in these terms even though there can be heated controversy between unions as to how groups should be represented and whether a particular member, or group of members, should be transferred to a different bargaining agent, or which union is the right and proper one in principle. This can be relevant if it involves the up-grading of, let us say, a fitter to a foreman's job – or a shift from the shop floor to staff status. Even at its most controversial this is never conducted on an *overtly* status-conscious basis.

In the course of this book we shall deal with the world as it presents itself now. White-collar workers will be either those who are already members of a white-collar union or who are eligible for membership and typically these will be people whose job titles come within the orbit of the New Earnings Survey list. There are exceptions to this on three grounds, none of which is statistically or analytically important. One is that some job titles are not included in the NES list; another is that in some cases generally acknowledged white-collar unions have a degree of manual worker membership; the third is the difficulty of defining a white-collar union. One definition used to be, quite unsatisfactorily, based on membership of the non-manual workers organisation within the TUC. But this has now been abolished on the grounds that a large proportion of the TUC membership is now in this category and it was absurd to sustain a patronised section. Without a working definition of white-collar workers, the difficulties start to multiply. There is an incredible lack of official or reliable data regarding the numbers and type of employees involved, the changes in the total workforce, and so on. There are some industry-wide surveys on employees, but it is impossible to argue generally from particular cases, especially in a swiftly changing industrial and national employment scene. The impact of the computer on employment is at best uncharted and there are serious questions as to whether the changes that have taken place up to now will be replicated with the new computer technologies. The other technological changes have also produced short-term effects whilst general governmental economic policy has had a very important effect on the distribution of employment. Of course such policies are reversible in political terms, but the technology is generally irreversible.

The economy of any industrialised nation can be reasonably divided into four main sectors; those of manufacturing, distribution, services and government, each of which make competing demands for resources including manpower. In some other countries agriculture would be included, but this does not represent a very high percentage of the UK labour force – at only 1·5 per cent in 1977. In general terms, the manufacturing sector employs a high percentage of manual workers as does distribution, whilst both the service and government sectors employ a far higher percentage of non-manual workers. Thus, any shift of emphasis in economic policy terms towards those latter sectors will equally mean a shift towards non-manual employment providing that the relative balance of manual to non-manual employees in each of the sectors remains substantially unchanged. A recent series of economic articles by Eltis and Bacon pointed to such a change having taken place over the last twenty years, thus the growth in numbers of the white-collar employees has been far higher than that of the labour force in general.

Although there is a dearth of information on manpower and its allocation, there exists the 1971 Census information. There is no definition of white-collar worker but the information is quite detailed on a 10 per cent sample basis. Jobs are analysed into groups and then within each group subdivided by job title. The Census defines five basic groups of interest: clerical workers; sales workers; service, sports and recreation; professional, technical and artists; administrative and managers. In addition there are, in a separate section, the managers, foremen (and women) outside these broad categories. Oddly many of the jobs subsumed in these categories could hardly be described as white-collar (cleaners, canteen aides and shelf stackers) although the details are sufficient to adjust for this, albeit in a purely subjective manner. The following data are thus not strictly accurate, but almost certainly accurate to within 1 or 2 per cent, given the general perception of a white-collar job.

In all, the Census traced nearly 22 million men and women who were employees, along with another 1·8 million self-employed people. Of the employed, 13·5 million were men and 8·4 million were women. We suspect however that the total number (especially where women are concerned) is an underestimate due to the fear that disclosure in the Census of either a part-time, or a second, job would incur increased personal tax liabilities. In the five groups with which we are concerned, there were 6·3 million men and 6·35 million women. However, after adjusting for manual jobs within the non-manual context, these were reduced to 5·9 million men and 4·1 million women or 43·7 per cent of all employed men and 49·2 per cent of all employed women. The larger percentage of women may well be due to the lack of information on female part-time manual work and home working and the very large proportion involved in clerical activities. Both sets of figures probably represent underestimates in that certain white-collar jobs in manually oriented manufacturing industries have been omitted from the data, but the difference will be marginal (we estimate) in the region of 1·5 per cent.

Of the white-collar employees there were 2·4 times as many women as men in clerical employment, nearly 11 times as many men as women in the administrative and managerial sections and 1·5 times as many men as women in the professional, technical and artists section. Some of the discrepancies between male and female employment are disturbing: 52,000 male as opposed to 13,100 female doctors, over 8,000 men with only 200 women working as metallurgists and 24,300 men but a mere 3,400 women as university teachers. The Sex Discrimination Act will have to be potent to eliminate these distinctions.

Female white-collar workers are marginally less likely to be married than all women workers – 62·4 per cent against 63 per cent. Those working in the administrative and managerial jobs are more likely to be single as only 54·8 per cent are married. Some of this difference is due to the fact that 34·2 per cent are single as opposed to the 28·3 per cent married women workers, but the rest is due to a higher divorced or widowed rate – 10·5 per cent as opposed to 8·7 per cent.

There are few age differentials between the non-manual and manual sections. As would be expected, managerial, foremen and professional sections have little or no representation under the age of twenty-four years, but this is balanced by the clerical section having a preponderance of employees under this age.

In geographical representation there is an acute imbalance. Scotland is very under-represented whilst the Greater London Area is over-represented. The South East region alone accounts for 44 per cent of male and 42 per cent of all female clerical staffs, whilst Greater London itself has almost 25 per cent of the entire country's clerical workers. Over 50 per cent of the female administrators and managers are in the South East, whilst only 43 per cent of male managers live there and 46 per cent of all professional and technical male employees are in the South East; yet, for women, the South East accounts for only 39 per cent. The next most important of the regions in terms of white-collar employment is the North West with roughly 12 per cent of both men and women. Taking the South East, the North West and the West Midlands together they account for seven out of ten of all male professional and technical staff and women administrators and managers and not less than six out of ten of any of the other major white-collar groups.

On examining these aggregate figures more closely there is much to support casual, broadly based assumptions. Women, who provide the overwhelming majority of clerical and teaching staffs are, not unnaturally, less concentrated in the three main regions except in the managerial grades. As teachers are found in all parts of the country, and clerical workers in all forms of economic and political activity, the greater dispersion of women is to be expected.

In the same way the head offices of companies and government departments tend to be concentrated in the South East. It is here that one expects to find the highest number of managerial and administrative staffs especially amongst the multinational companies. Obviously, plant and line management and foremen and supervisors are to be found wherever the productive processes are found and in these job categories the numbers in the South East are lower than the average of 45·8 per cent in all the categories mentioned. This short profile of where white-collar workers are located and their concentrations does not, however, represent the main and most interesting phenomenon: their relative and absolute growth within the labour force as a whole.

In 1910 there were just over 3·3 million white-collar members; by 1971 there were over 10 million, and in this period the total labour force expanded by less than 40 per cent. In terms of numbers the blue-collar workers have thus stayed almost static over this period, although their proportion of the labour force has dwindled from just over 75 per cent to currently less than 55 per cent. This change, although over a sixty-year period, has accelerated since 1945 and, more especially, in the past fifteen years.

From 1959 to 1974 the total of local government employees rose by over 66 per cent and, although not all of these are white-collar, a very significant percentage fall into recognisable non-manual categories. Banking, insurance and finance staffs generally rose to over 1·1 million (this was an increase of over 74 per cent and nearly all of these were white-collar); market research employed 71 per cent more people; business services went up by a staggering 321 per cent and central offices rose by 147 per cent. To put this acceleration into its true perspective: in 1907, 8 per cent of the labour force was white-collar; by 1966 this had reached 24 per cent, yet in the five years to 1971 this had risen to over 45 per cent and by this year may be approaching the 50 per cent mark for the first time. The DoE has published a study of the labour market by 1981 which indicates that this growth rate will be maintained. The total increase in the labour force from 1961 to 1981 is expected to be from 23·2 to 25 million, yet the increase in administrators, managers, professional and technology employees is expected to be from 2·7 million to 5·8 million or an increase of 116 per cent. The service, sport and recreation sector, although not all white-collar (as in the previous classification), is expected to grow from 2·4 million to 3·3 million or an increase of 35·6 per cent. The growth in the other sectors which typically employ a high percentage of non-manual workers is just as large. This study estimates that the compound-growth rate of the working population between 1971 and 1981 will be 0·4 per cent, whilst public services will use 1 per cent more labour, public administration 1·4 per cent, insurance and banking 2·6 per cent, health 3·2 per cent and, finally, education employment in all forms will increase by 3·4 per cent. As with many government statistics, however, these are suspect in that they are based on compilations of poor data and do not take into account some new factors such as micro-computers.

Britain is changing dramatically as far as the composition of its labour force is concerned. Whereas in the recent past the manual, or blue-collar, workers were in the forefront in absolute numbers, in percentage terms and in union-organisation terms the positions look likely to be reversed by the very early 1980s. The political implications of this change can hardly be over-stated while the reasons for this very dramatic change are imperfectly understood and the subject of considerable debate and disagreement. It is noticeable that when compared with the US, Germany and Japan, the growth in British service-sector employment in the decade from 1961 was not all that startling with 14·6 per cent in the UK, 19·2 per cent in Japan, 12·6 per cent in West Germany and 9·3 per cent in the USA (only the USA had a higher percentage employed in this sector). The difference lies in the employment situation in the manufacturing sector. In the UK this sector employed 12·5 per cent fewer people over the same decade, whilst West Germany employed 2 per cent more, Japan 21 per cent more and the USA only 0·66 per cent fewer. In each of the other three countries there has been a large drift from the agricultural sector in comparison with Britain.

The percentage growth of service industries of all descriptions is thus moderately uniform in industrialised market economies, but the difference in Britain is the run-down of employment in the manufacturing sector. This run-down then changes the relative percentage of those employed with the service sector employing a considerably higher percentage of white-collar workers. As a result, in Britain we have a higher overall portion of the working population doing what are classed as white-collar jobs.

Traditionally it has always been assumed that as technological advances make the manufacturing industries more capital intensive, and thus labour requirements are cut, so the service sector will absorb those whose services are no longer required. This theory has an earlier parallel in the drift from agricultural employment to manufacturing during the industrial revolution. To get technological innovation, one needs investment, yet Britain is lagging well behind its competitors in this area. The drive towards white-collar employment has come at the expense of the manufacturing sector, but not as a result of its increased efficiency. It is interesting, for example, to note that Britain has only 42·7 per cent of employees in the manufacturing sector, whilst West Germany has 50·4 per cent. It is impossible for a nation such as Britain, which depends on exporting manufactured goods to pay for food and raw material imports, to continue to run down its manufacturing sector and still be able to purchase enough goods from abroad. This argues for a radical change in economic policies which may well alter the forecasts of white-collar employment.

Admittedly the new manufacturing sector must be capital intensive, but until such time as governments encourage the demand for services to rise, the service sector will be unable to 'mop-up' those made redundant. Unless government itself employs these people, the trend towards an increase in white-collar employment will slow down over the years to the early 1980s. There is no substantial agricultural sector on which to call, although this is a sector in which our industrialised competitors still have a substantial workforce.

Having stated this, it is still likely that by 1985 at the latest, at least 50 per cent of the workforce will be performing 'non-manual' labour. Jobs not previously in existence will become a reality as technological changes create new demands for increased expertise and these jobs will almost certainly be in the non-manual, technician areas. Skilled trades, such as lathe operating or welding, have already been hit by the introduction of automated techniques and all the evidence points to an increasing diminution in the use of such skills in industry and a lowering of the demand (although to not such a great extent) for semi-skilled and unskilled labour. Conversely, it is likely that any manufacturing, industry-based expansion will rely on employees with some qualifications in increasing numbers and that these new skills will replace the older, either dying or eliminated crafts. In trade union membership terms this will have most important repercussions.

Britain is not only a class-ridden society, but also a very status-ridden community. We have neither a meritocratic system using money or prestige as the recognition factor, nor a social-usefulness system, nor a caste system nor a really effective 'old boy network'. What is in evidence is a hodge-podge of salaries and status, none of which has been consciously formulated, but which has grown out of the labour-relations system or its inadequacies over the last one hundred years. Status is certainly not based on earnings. Nursing, a traditionally low paid occupation, has always been a high-status occupation and whilst a Ford foreman can earn in excess of £9,000 a year (prompting a Merseyside

works notice-board mock headline: *Ford Foreman Marries Commoner*)
he or she has a far lower status than a computer programmer earning
£4,000 per annum.

Status is still a state of mind. It is rather like the classic economic
theory of utility function, made up of individual elements, ranked in
some subconscious order of merit, like dirty hands, or who you mix
with at work. But the in-work environment or at the least the in-work
conditions of service play a more important part in in-work status than
is widely appreciated. Apart from the normal conditions such as
holidays, pension, car, mortgage facilities, etc., there are the factors of
whether an office is shared, or whether there is sole access to a secretary;
is there carpeting, or a picture on the wall; which lavatory can be used
and which canteen can be used; a host of subtle, in-work distinctions,
each of which, although trivial in itself, adds up to status. Status distinction has been used in Britain to a very sophisticated degree. The honours
system, from the Royal Victorian Order, Third-class, to the Garter, is
mimicked in industrial relations where it has been used in lieu of
income. It provides a differential over and above other employees
which costs the employer as little as possible whilst satisfying the
recipient as much as possible. For the most part this book is taken up
with the gradual undermining of this posture and the repercussions
thereof.

Job titles play their part in this status game. For nigh on fifty years
there has been a subtle distinction between supervisor and foreman,
technician and technical assistant, research associate and assistant and
so on. Employees have literally had, as part of their remuneration, the
ability to announce and trade on a significant-sounding title at social
gatherings or, importantly, when applying for another job. *The job title
is a tyranny in itself.* Employees are tied to a title which only too often
bears little relationship to the work actually being done. What, for
example, is a foreman or a systems analyst? What are the functions,
duties and responsibilities of such jobs? What qualifications are needed
and how much experience for either job? The answers vary enormously
depending on the type of plant or installation, on the internal structure,
and on the money differentials operating within the enterprise. There
are no easy, discreet answers.

This, however, is important. A new job may be within reach if the
title of the previous job was right, or the title rather than the job being
done might well bring with it the deference of other employees or
neighbours in a knowing community. Employees have been locked into
their jobs by the title. On the one hand it was impossible to get short-
listed for a new job and on the other the status was too much to lose.
Job titles and the minuscule distinctions that go with them are probably
more important in the white-collar areas than in the manual-worker

spheres. With an apparently unlimited promotional vista once on the staff, the nuances of the pecking order become that much more important. The tyranny is inherent in both the tying effect and the substitute remuneration aspect. For example 'senior whatsoever' has no entitlement to overtime, only the 'deputy whatsoever' can be paid for work actually done. In addition, management, or at least management-type job-titled employees, do not join unions. Unions are for those who cannot advance, who cannot influence, who can afford the luxury of outside affiliations, or so the theory used to go. Fortunately, for those in this position, this theory is becoming less relevant as companies pay less attention to detail and more to the title; fortunately, the result is an increase in trade union membership in the whole area and this brings with it a developing objectivity.

If the number of white-collar employees has increased remarkably over the last decade, so the number of potential members of the white-collar trade unions has commensurately increased. Union penetration is, by and large, lower than in the blue-collar areas for reasons of ethos, class, management pressure and lack of resources within the unions themselves to channel and harness the needs and energies of the potential recruits. There has, however, been growth in the white-collar union part of the trade union movement. It is growth that is reflected in membership levels, but not yet acquisition of power within the movement itself. Before long their recruitment area will encompass over half of the working population and union strength will reflect this. The changes that this will inevitably bring to the life of Britain, its industry and commerce, government and not the least its trade union movement will be radical in the extreme. One thing is certain, an employee whether he or she is white-collar, blue-collar or professional, is an employee, and given injustice and a perspective and given the system prevailing at present will be militant when the occasion arises. As the middle class expands, or its collectivisation accelerates, so trade unions will expand with it. As the expansion is almost certainly into the high technological industries and the services that these then create, it is the white-collar union that will be the union of the future.

Chapter 2

The rise and short history of white-collar unionism

'The people arose as one man.' – Judges

A revealing facet of the mass movement of salaried staffs into unions is that it has been against the stream of media criticism. The recent past has seen a growing wave of attack, some informed but the majority blatantly prejudiced, centred in the national, popular press. This reached a crescendo in the period preceding the Industrial Relations Act, 1970, was blunted by that Act's ineffectiveness and re-emerged in late 1973. Having fought and lost a General Election based on the 1973/4 miners' strike and the associated 'Who rules Britain?' issue, both the Conservative Party and the printed media were unnerved and changed tactics. A softer, subtler approach is now in evidence; union election procedures are now the target in a campaign of suggestion to union members that they are merely lambs being misled by politically motivated rogue sheep.

The interesting, indeed fascinating, factor is that in this period trade union membership grew at a faster rate than at any other time since the early part of this century and the immediate post-Second World War years, and did so within a diminishing total labour force. In the light of this strange juxtaposition of events, facile explanations carry little credence.

The need to protect incomes against inflation was an important but not a dominating motive. From the evidence of meetings and the bursts of recruitment activity, it appears that most people take no notice of the media, or rather their repeated advice – a view that can be reinforced by the election of Labour governments in the face of an almost universally hostile press. It could be that the British are more radical than is generally supposed and that the vilifying campaign had the positive effect of recruiting people. This would be pleasing to believe, but is almost certainly fanciful. It may be that most employees now know some active trade unionists personally and realise that the descriptions of them in the media bear no relationship to their personal experiences and perceptions. Alternatively it may well have been that the underlying social and economic conditions in this period were *so* conducive to trade union growth that they overcame the media's pressures. The answer is most probably a combination of these and yet other factors because, despite the hostile environment, despite the Industrial Relations Act, and despite the smaller pond in which to fish, trade unions made great advances in membership and prestige. Foremost in contibuting to this growth were the non-manual employees, whether joining a basically manual workers' union or a specifically up-market, white-collar union.

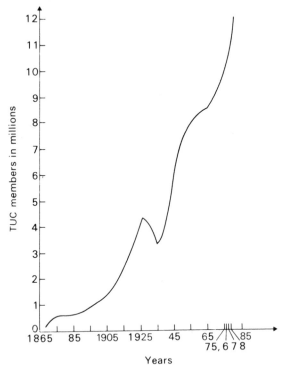

Figure 2.1. TUC membership 1868–1977

The trade union movement grew out of the Industrial Revolution. As industries developed, so the migration from the countryside into the growing towns accelerated; new processes superseded the old and the domestic and employment conditions of those at work worsened. The individual worker was totally at the mercy of his or her employer and the only possible response, short of a political revolution, was to build up the trade union movement as a countervailing force against employers. Not unnaturally, given the structure of the economy and the labour force, the earliest trade unions were based on crafts, skills, narrow industries and companies. To all intents and purposes there was no government sector, nor indeed other than the retail and wholesale trades, a services and leisure sector. The number of non-direct, non-productive employees was very low, both in absolute numbers and as a percentage of the labour force as a whole, so that in this respect it was natural for the membership of the earlier unions to be exclusively manual workers. Recruitment and organisation in these unions was hampered by a series of adverse and hostile employers as well as judicial and legislative decisions and took place against a background of bitter disputes. In these early days when remuneration was so low and profits so high, working conditions so hazardous and children both worked and slept in the factories, these disputes were, literally, about life and death matters.

The non-directly productive employees of this era were totally unorganised and worked in company offices as clerks, for local councils, in the Civil Service, in solicitors' offices, for publishers or as teachers. There were very few managers, only owners and workers. They were small in numbers and economic influence, although politically of great importance to the emergent entrepreneurs. Although the remuneration was only marginally higher for the majority of these employees, there was a very marked status difference between the manual workers and the office worker. Rules governing time-keeping were less stringent, the working environment was far less harsh; longer holidays existed, sometimes sick pay and hours of work were shorter. So, the white-collar employee was basically management-orientated, was viewed as an extension of management and never as an employee or fellow worker. Although in some cases, such as loom overlookers, there were early rudimentary organisations of non-manual workers, these only applied to the production workers' supervisors whose function was to work on the shop floor and not to those whose jobs kept them physically separated from manual workers. In this period white-collar workers viewed themselves as groups apart, neither wanting nor needing trade union representation but relying instead on patronage and paternalism. This still provides a premium. This state of affairs changed as the patterns of employment changed, but very slowly indeed. In the private sector those companies which were divided into 'works' and 'staff' found little if any impetus towards unionisation amongst the 'staff' personnel, but in the emerging sectors such as the railways where there were no old status barriers in the workplace, white-collar unionism rooted more readily. At the same time, successive governments took on more responsibilities and the Civil Service expanded stimulating union growth in this sector.

This distinction between the early rate of growth of white-collar union consciousness is both interesting and important. Certainly there were more non-manual employees in the non-physical output sectors, engaged as railway clerks, booking clerks, secretaries and clerks in the Civil Service, and school teachers, at a time when the private manufacturing company had not yet grown to a size needing the services of the thousands of back-up staff needed today. Allowing for this, there were still some employers of substantial numbers of 'white-collar' workers in insurance companies, banks, some large companies in shipbuilding and steel production and the City employees of the large trading companies. Yet, despite the fact that recruitment for nearly all of these jobs required similar qualifications and similar skills, there was a remarkably skewed growth of the white-collar unions. If it was the prevailing local ethos to join, why did the clerical staff and supervisory staff in highly manually unionised companies not organise, because the background of those employed in the offices was very similar if not identical to those on the shop floor? Why should railway booking office clerks or teachers organise effectively earlier than insurance staffs; if status considerations applied to one as they probably did in (say) a shipbuilding yard, why did they not apply to the other?

One prerequisite for trade union organisation is a commonwealth of interest amongst those eligible to join and another is a sufficiency of numbers employed by the same employer. Teachers and civil servants certainly met both criteria, whilst the average clerk working for a manufacturing company found neither. The bank or insurance company clerk probably not only lacked the common interest, in that their jobs varied markedly at that time, but the companies themselves were still small and personalised. Equally, unless there was a catastrophic failure, such employees tended to be insulated from the cycle of boom and slump far more than the manufacturing sector and their salaries were marginally higher. Growth was thus unequal.

When the TUC first met in 1868 there were thirty-four delegates representing 118,000 workers, none of whom were white collar, although there was at least one white-collar union in existence in the shape of the NUET which was founded in 1860. It took until 1970 for the NUT to affiliate to the TUC.

In the years following, to the turn of the century, white-collar workers organised slowly and painfully in small numbers. In 1881 the Association of Post Office Telegraphists, five years later came the Post Office Clerks and just creeping into the twentieth century, the Railway Clerks. Other small local unions existed, especially in the textile industries, but these had functions more compatible with those of Friendly Societies than those we now associate with trade union work.

The classic, traditional trade union movement represented, not surprisingly, the industries which had made Britain 'great'. Coal, iron and steel, wool and cotton, railways and shipbuilding were pre-eminent, and these, along with the dockers and railwaymen, were the driving forces behind the movement. The unions themselves were usually small and fragmented and mainly based as their names imply, on trades rather than industries. This, like most social developments, was illogical, given the problems confronting the workers. The carding room in a mill had health hazards associated with the inhaling of dry fibre, resulting in an appallingly high incidence of lung disease, whilst the loomsheds themselves were 'steamed' to maintain humidity which led to major respiratory casualties. Yet opposition to both practices was inhibited by having separate unions, indeed many unions were divided, not only by specific skill, but also by district. Divide and rule is a well tried and very successful tactic, yet employers had no need to use it: the early unions did it all for them because they did not have the resources or capacity to mount overall strategies.

Trade union membership continued to grow and by 1900 there were 176 separate unions affiliated to the TUC of which four, the life assurance agents at the Prudential, the musicians, the loom overlookers and the shop assistants, warehousemen and clerks could be considered to be white collar. The ensuing period to the start of the First World War was the climacteric of Britain's economic performance and power, but it was still based on the traditional industrial sectors and the overwhelming growth of the giant combines had yet to start. Crafts and trades still ruled the roost and did so until Henry Ford revolutionised productive processes by initiating mass-production techniques. By 1914 there were over 2,600,000 union members in 195 TUC-affiliated unions. The white-collar representation, although it had grown remarkably in respect of the numbers of organisations, was still numerically very small. There were fourteen white-collar unions, of which the largest was the Railway Clerks, but the representation had now spread into mining, the theatre, the post office, and a remarkable expansion of insurance unions (there were now four). At the same time, other organisations existed outside the TUC: the local government officials and civil servants both had thriving non-TUC-affiliated, but very representative, organisations.

War years are always considered good for trade union recruitment. Trade unions, despite all propaganda to the contrary, are a very important element in industrial harmony and peace. More to the point, managements generally realise this. In wartime, when there is pressure for maximum production, employers have generally encouraged union membership, either overtly or by not opposing it. The First World War was no exception and by 1918 the TUC could count 5,283,000 members in over 240 affiliated bodies: a membership almost precisely doubled from the start to the end of the war. It has been estimated that another one million employees were members of non-TUC-affiliated bodies. The war had a critical effect on the composition of the labour force. For the first time women entered into competition with men for jobs and were no longer totally confined to the mills or the kitchen as sources of mass employment. By the end of the war there were eighteen solely white-collar unions as TUC affiliates and some of them were reaching for significant memberships. Leaving aside the railways, the clerks had 28,000 members, post office engineers 15,000, school teachers 7,000 and there were 16,000 musicians. For the first time tax clerks were affiliated and at this point in time so were prison officers.

The 1920s and 1930s were not good times for the economy, for the trade union movement or for employment. New productive techniques started to nibble at the dominance of the craftsman and brought in their wake industrial re-organisation and the start of the trend towards industrial concentration. In turn this meant that in the manufacturing sectors, units became larger and the scope for recruitment amongst the emerging numbers of clerical, administrative, supervisory, technical and general back-up staff in turn became larger, although the prospect of one man waiting for another's job was enough to daunt all but the most committed pioneer.

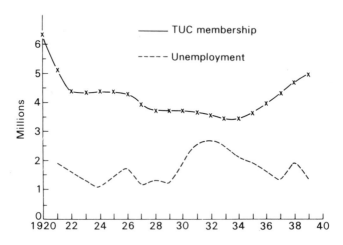

Figure 2.2. Comparison of TUC membership and unemployment 1920–39

However, this was precisely the period when the white-collar unions were first officially acknowledged by the TUC as a group meriting special attention. In 1924 a Congress non-manual workers' advisory committee was formed, along with the NFPW, and a new TUC section for 'non-manuals' was created for affiliates. In 1925 there were eight unions in it with a combined membership of 62,000 of which two insurance unions claimed 25,000. This membership, representing only 1·3 per cent of the potential, was nothing like a really fair representation of the pace of white-collar unionism. Seven unions in the public sector section added another 45,000; railway clerks (then in the private sector) with 66,000 were by far the largest of the white-collar unions; the draughtsmen's union which had just obtained national recognition from the engineering employers had 11,000; the NFA, a forerunner of the ASSET and then the ASTMS, had 2,000 and the colliery and textile industry white-collar unions added another 45,000. Thus, by 1925 there were over twenty TUC-affiliated white-collar unions which had roughly 5 per cent of the total membership. It is interesting to note that at this time the white-collar unions outside the TUC were almost equal in numbers to those inside.

The 1930s were a time of unmitigated working-class misery. By 1935 total TUC membership had dropped to just over 3·6 million, the non-manual section had dropped to seven affiliates with only 54,000 members of whom 30,000 were in the insurance industry. The public sector union affiliation had dwindled, too – Civil Service unions had been forced to drop out by post-General Strike legislation. The embryo draughtsmen's union, the AESD, however increased its membership to nearly 18,000 and became the white-collar pacemaker in the metal-working industries. (The Second World War had the same effect on union membership as had the First. Even foremen, represented by ASSET, were able, after a prolonged struggle, to obtain recognition from the EEF and started to increase in membership in spite of concerted resistance by companies.) By 1924, TUC membership had risen to over seven and a half million, the non-manual section's affiliates were now twelve with 204,000 members. The white-collar unions continued to recruit. The AESD had 41,000, the Clerical and Administrative Workers Union had 32,000, the insurance agents had 41,000, while the Civil Service and public sector white-collar unions totalled another 400,000 albeit most outside the TUC.

White-collar union strength was clearly growing, slowly in the private sector, but fast in public employment, for it was precisely here that jobs were being created. The nationalised industries, the Civil Service (almost doubling its non-industrial staff in the seven years since the start of the war) and local government, were all growing and recruiting. The concept of the welfare state and the introduction of the NHS both added to white-collar employment. This was because the ethos of the public sector was benevolent towards collective bargaining as it had been since J. H. Whitley's report in 1919 on the future of labour relations, commissioned by Lloyd George to head off labour unrest.

Nationalisation also boosted organisation although not all the new managements were especially sympathetic. Nevertheless, they had statutory duties laid upon them by the relevant nationalising acts to recognise and consult with appropriate unions. The new public corporations' staffs were there in large numbers, with a common employer and varying terms and conditions of service crying out for rationalisation. The unions happily assessed and shouldered the detailed task.

The 1950s saw a consolidation of this trend. Although steel and road transport were mainly de-nationalised, the trade union membership stuck. The immediate post-war reconstruction gave way to the 'you have never had it so good' era. The terms of trade were mainly in Britain's favour, newer industries started to emerge – petro-chemicals, pharmaceuticals, plastics, artificial fibres and electrical goods – whilst the traditional industries such as coal mining, the railways and textile manufacturing started their rapid decline. At the same time the first large mergers were taking place; take-overs and larger companies were starting to be in vogue, multinational corporations (mainly American) started to move into the UK even more strongly. The economic, political and social conditions were far removed from the 1930s, and the pattern of employment was beginning to reflect the change.

In 1953 the TUC had 184 affiliated organisations with almost 8·1 million members and a visibly expanding white-collar section. The bank employees had joined with 36,000 members, the draughtsmen now had 55,000 members, ASSET 15,000, CAWU over 40,000. TSSA (the old railway clerks) peaked at 90,000 and the Civil Service and Post Office white-collar unions claimed over 300,000. The composition of the TUC was starting to change in a most radical fashion. It is still worthwhile remembering unions were not only recruiting but recruiting very quickly and had built up roughly another 400,000 members, although they in most cases, together with the teachers, stood on the sidelines.

The growth in the white-collar unions was still very much in the public sector. Although unions primarily based on private manufacturing had increased their membership, the Civil Service and Post Office provided the main growth. Furthermore, the private sector unions were very naturally based in the old trade or craft style – clerks, draughtsmen, supervisors – industry-based like the NUBE or the UIS. Nothing resembling a white-collar general union was on the horizon. There were, however, other unions which some white-collar employees joined and these were basically manual-worker oriented. In the NHS, nurses joined NUPE or COHSE, the shop workers (USDAW) recruited pharmacists and the larger manual unions, NUGMW, and AUEW and the electricians started white-collar sections, whilst the TGWU clerical section founded in the 1920s began to expand marginally.

By 1967 there were 2·5 million non-manual workers in TUC-affiliated unions and in 1969, with roughly the same global figure, there were an estimated 800,000 of them in the private sector, a penetration of roughly only 13 per cent. 1977, the latest available year for which there are complete statistics, showed that the trend was continuing to accelerate. There were forty-four unions which could be described as white collar with a membership of 3·3 million employees; in addition, another four on the border-line took the total to over 3 million. However, adding in all the non-manual members of basically manual-worker unions, there were over 4·6 million non-manual members in seventy-five different unions.

The last decade has not only seen this large growth in middle-class unionisation, it has also seen a corresponding growth in academic investigation of the phenomenon. Certainly some unions seem to have taken off and indeed the whole white-collar element has expanded. This is, of course, exaggerated by simply assessing TUC figures. NALGO, now Britain's fourth largest union, affiliated to the TUC in 1964, and the Society of Civil Servants in 1973, followed by the Association of University Teachers and the Institution of Professional Civil Servants in 1976 and the First Division Association in 1977. These have had substantial membership for many years, and the growth they appear to have engendered in Congress figures is only real in the case of NALGO.

Although the growth is still uneven, there are signs that the private sector is starting to respond. ASTMS (which grew by generalised recruitment, and the absorption of other organisations of which only five were TUC affiliates) has over 440,000 members and is a general union; APEX (the re-titled Clerical and Administrative Workers Union) has 150,000; TASS (the draughtsmen) has 178,000; NUBE 117,000, with ACTSS (the white-collar section of the TGWU) claiming 122,000 members, most of whom are private sector. Nevertheless, the Civil Service unions alone account for 530,000, NALGO has 709,000 and teachers, polytechnic teachers and university teachers another 532,000. The public sector white-collar unions still dominate the whole grouping in membership, but probably not in economic leverage. Nevertheless, by 1977, over 38 per cent of all TUC members could be defined as white-collar (on a very conservative definition) and this percentage has almost certainly increased since then as some unions lost members (these are the basic craft or industry unions), but TUC membership continues to increase. The probability is that by 1980 the percentage will be in the 42 per cent range and by 1985 over 50 per cent. This underlines the central importance to the TUC, and unions generally, of continued penetration in these fields.

These are not idle speculations. As we have seen, the DoE projection of the labour force composition shows an increasing catchment area for the white-collar sector at the expense of the manual sector and this,

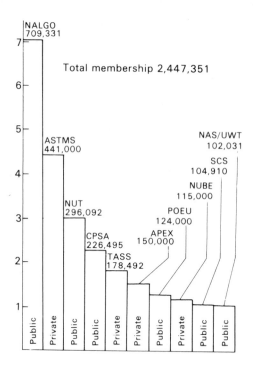

Figure 2.3. The ten largest white-collar unions, 1977

combined with the probability of increased unionisation of women following reform legislation, should, if anything, make this prediction of union membership to be on the conservative side. The changes in membership are slowly being reflected in the composition of the General Council of the TUC and in its approach to the membership. The non-manual workers' advisory conference was wound up in 1975 because it was inappropriate for such a large minority to be catered for in such a way, and also because any problems which did arise were so substantial as to demand attention from the standard Congress machinery. The non-manual workers advisory committee disappeared for the same reason, that there was now no longer a need to provide a specific non-manual representative forum. Of a General Council of forty members, nine or ten of these (depending on definitions) can be defined as being representative of white-collar unions. In 1974 an extra seat had to be allocated to the Technical and Scientific Group because of its increased membership and in 1977 an extra seat awarded to the Civil Service/Post Office Group. This representation will change again as total TUC membership changes.

Thus, academic investigations have concentrated on finding a reason for this growth and development. Propositions put forward have been disingenuous or simply portray it all as a reaction to inflation and incomes policies. The theory held for the longest time (and still holding) is that of Professor George Bain and is deeply concerned with recognition. It asserts that union growth follows recognition granted by an employer, and that government policies have played a great part in producing this recognition, either directly or indirectly. We shall discuss recognition later in this book, but in principle we believe there is substantial merit in it. It probably under-acknowledges the type of union without a nationally bargained agreement and the industrial disputes rather than the government aid which led to recognition. It also tends to ignore the original growth in membership which has to precede recognition.

There is no single reason, but recognition which stabilises and legitimises a union presence is central. But why, after recognition, have some unions grown so much faster than others, given equal recruitment areas? Why did ASSET, which had EEF recognition in 1944, have to wait until the 1960s for its take-off?

One singular example may show that the world is not always reducible to simple, all-embracing theories. This is the case of the 'Foreman and Staff Mutual Benefit Society'. This was a Friendly Society which provided sick benefits, death benefits, unemployment benefits, pensions and endowment benefits to 'foremen, underforemen and all employees holding positions of trust or employment on the management, technical, office and commercial staffs and who have attained the age of 21'. In 1967 there were over 60,000 members employed at 2,700 different companies. All very laudable except for two reasons. These were rules seven and eleven of the Society, which precluded membership to any member of a trade union and furthermore, stated that if a current member of the Society joined a union, he or she would forfeit the right to any benefit and this included a forfeit of the member's own contributions! The EEF kept at hands' length from the FSMBS but supplied many support services and encouragement, sometimes sharing offices and officers.

The fund, which at that time was holding nearly £18 million of assets, was being used to prevent the unionisation of all staff, but mainly foremen in the engineering industry. After much legal advice, ASSET (as it then was) realised that only an Act of Parliament could change this situation. Several attempts had been made through the Private Member's bill system to deal with the situation, but the system in the Commons is such that this form of approach rarely reaches fruition. Both the Prices and Incomes Board and Lord Donovan's Commission on Trade Unions and Employers' Organisations came out firmly against this form of anti-trade union coercion and it was on this basis that ASSET, later in the proceedings to become ASTMS after its merger, decided to promote its own bill.

The union first had to change its rules so that it could 'promote legislation in Parliament for the benefit of its members'. It drafted a bill, had it approved by the membership as a whole, and then had to present the bill to a scrutiny committee of two Conservative and two Labour MPs who voted three to one on its acceptance. However, the FSMBS objected to the bill in Scotland (where it had its head office) and it took some considerable constitutional manoeuvrings to ensure that the bill, by now in the name of ASTMS, was presented to the House of Commons for a second reading. The Society still continued to oppose and a plan was laid for its rejection by certain Conservative MPs. After speeches by, amongst others, Russell Kerr and Fred Willey (both ASTMS-sponsored Labour MPs) the bill was passed by 125 to 9 (one of the opponents was Enoch Powell). It then went to a Committee where (among others) Professor Bain testified in its favour. The procedure for a bill of this nature is that it had to be independently introduced into the House of Lords. At this time the FSMBS suddenly dropped their opposition. The bill itself merely exempted ASTMS members from the provisions of rules seven and eleven. But this was enormously significant.

The under-publicised coup had the effect of stimulating an ASTMS 'take-off' in the engineering industry, as the financial penalty for potential members was removed. It also meant that apart from ASTMS

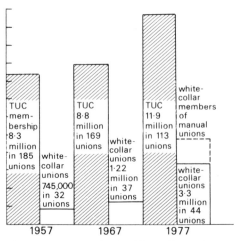

Figure 2.4. Growth of white-collar union membership (not including white-collar memberships of manual-worker unions in 1957 or 1967)

being the only union ever to have used this parliamentary procedure, the union became convinced that relatively unorthodox but highly sophisticated tactics could be made to work. In addition, it does show that although recognition is important, other factors play their part in fostering white-collar union growth (or in arresting it).

Of the 4·6 million white-collar workers who are members of TUC-affiliated trade unions, roughly only 1 million are in white-collar unions which deal with the private sector, whilst there are probably another 400,000 in the private sector (including nationalised industries) who belong to basically manual-worker unions. The specialist unions themselves have grown to some considerable size as we have seen earlier in the chapter. Although this is in itself an impressive achievement, it is the growth of this membership in the last two decades which is so significant. Let us compare the years 1957, 1967 and 1977 and, in particular, the last ten years.

Over the past two decades the number of white-collar union members belonging exclusively to white-collar unions has risen by 338 per cent. In number terms, the total TUC membership has increased by 3·6 million members and the white-collar sector alone by 2·5 million. If the non-manual members of white-collar unions are included, this increase is nearer to 3·1 million. This increase is shown dramatically when looking at the membership of a selection of TUC-affiliated unions.

It is clear that nearly all white-collar unions have grown in membership and more especially so over the last ten years. The two exceptions are the NUIW which represents insurance salesmen (a declining part of an expanding industry) and TSSA (part of a declining industry – the railways). However, this latest membership has now started to increase for reasons which we shall deal with in a later chapter.

Counterpointed with these increases have been the decrease in membership of the old-established industry unions. Between them the NUR and NUM lost just over 600,000 members as a result of rationalisations, whilst over the same twenty years ASTMS, TASS, APEX and NUBE – all predominantly private sector unions – increased their membership by almost the same amount. The more recently affiliated public sector unions, such as NALGO, NUT and CPSA, total well over 1 million more alone. The other major growth unions, such as NUPE, COHSE and USDAW, all have substantial white-collar membership and it is clear that there has been a radical change in composition of the labour force which over the last ten years has been reflected in trade union membership.

It is also clear that within sectors, there have been differential rates of increase in size. This tends to argue that the single-course growth theory is deficient in important respects. Obviously industry and sector conditions vary, but it seems reasonable to suppose that where a free choice is exercisable by potential members there are certain factors which make certain unions more attractive. It would seem equally reasonable to suppose that one such factor, an important one, would be the ability to be seen as a successful union. That is to say, generally meeting the members' aspirations.

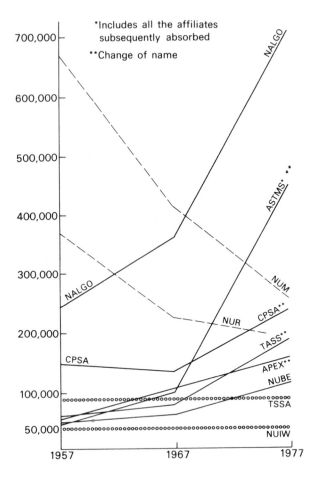

Figure 2.5. Growth in membership of selected unions, 1957–77

Price and Bain (University of Warwick), however, have different statistics on white-collar union membership and densities. They include all bodies, staff associations, etc. By 1974 they calculated that white-collar union membership was 4·26 million accounting for 36·3 per cent of all union membership and a density of 39·4 per cent. However, they are including a total of 1·3 million people who are in bodies not affiliated to the TUC, almost all of whom they are adding to the white-collar total. Some of these have since affiliated whilst others would not qualify as trade unions (in the authors' opinion).

On the other side of the coin, the disparity of white-collar union membership and the multiplicity of the unions themselves suggests that growth in this sector as a whole was due to overall national and international pressures of a general nature. The catch-all word 'white collar' conceals as large a range of job titles, job descriptions and industries as does 'manual workers'. A foreman in a small engineering plant, a consultant surgeon, a tax inspector, a scientist, an actuary, a copy typist, a computer programmer or a council clerk have little, if anything, in common. Education, job requirements and background are in all probability very different (if anything far more different than those in manual employments) yet they are often treated as a single, homogeneous entity by the press and by academics. It is very similar to the academic economist who starts with 'let us assume perfect competition' and goes on to produce an elegant theory but one which is rooted firmly in anything but reality. As trade union officers we have developed a thesis based on our experience.

First, there has been the change in the labour force that we referred to earlier and this has obviously not only provided a larger catchment area for the white-collar unions, but diminished that of the manual workers' unions. Then there has been the growth of the giant employers. Local government, the NHS and government departments have all been re-organised over the last ten years on the basis that big is good and, it would appear, the bigger the better.

In the private sector the sixties was the decade of the take-over, the conglomerate, the multinational and the asset stripper. Giant companies such as GEC, BLMC and Courtaulds were freshly constituted, expanded and consolidated; the conglomerate holding company (for example, Thomas Tilling with companies in transport, insurance, artificial limbs and ceramics) sprang up; the multinational established itself and grew as technology gave market entry to only those companies who could finance the expensive central research; and finally the asset stripper threatened as he collected, dissected and discarded diverse companies.

This trend had two major effects on white-collar employees. The first was to remove the personal contact with those higher up the management chain whilst, simultaneously, making it clear that control and authority had passed into hands which were remote both physically and politically. The second was uncertainty. A major motivating force in Britain, now prevalent amongst the middle classes, is the concept of security and the possibility of a 'career'. Many jobs, though apparently dull on the surface, have the advantage of good pensions and continuity of employment; thus life can be planned to some degree and in the hope of comfort. The changes in structure removed this security in the private sector and the predictability in the public sector. Redundancies, hitherto not dreamt of in the white-collar field, hit hard (GEC staffs were in one such organisation) and both managerial and white-collar unemployment became a serious problem in the late 1960s and early 1970s.

Mergers in banking, insurance, shipping as well as manufacturing all had their effect. Equally unsettling were the new demands, in newly formed corporate structures, made of personnel who did not really know what was expected of them. As the companies became larger, so it became more likely that job evaluations would be made and staff for the first time realised that they personally would have no bargaining position and that the die would be cast, with or without their approval. The unilateral power of some great companies to manage without check had become multiplied.

All this did not mean that employees suddenly rushed out to telephone a local union office and say 'I must join, I'm isolated, alienated, insecure and helpless'. What did happen was that people were jerked out of their previously entrenched psychological positions and forced to confront the reality that they, too, were employees, every bit as much as a worker on a production line. Even now this is not generally acknowledged publicly or overtly. For some people, the impending redundancies were enough to stimulate union membership; for some others smaller local difficulties (job evaluation for example) due to re-organisations forced employees into trade unions in order to retaliate, to bargain. For the most part, however, the uncertainties and change of employment conditions acted as a catalyst generally. Technological advance also played its part in stimulating uncertainties and a resultant change of mood. Where, before, careers were mapped out and employees did not join a union for fear of management reprisals, changes in techniques (notably computers) made skills redundant and downgraded jobs. Employees who for twenty years had coped well with the tasks in hand were suddenly confronted with a totally new set of instructions and worried as to whether they could cope – and what would happen to them if it were seen that they could not.

What all white-collar employees have in common is some notion of status. They expect some form of monetary reward for this. One major factor in white-collar union growth has been the erosion of the reward, that is to say differentials have been narrowing between them and the manual workers. What was worse was that some groups, such as radiographers and other paramedical staffs, suddenly realised how far behind they lagged. This, combined with loss of power or authority within larger units, give a fillip to unionisation. For example, the consultants are at least as much concerned at their loss of power in the reorganised NHS as they are about private practice; and the junior hospital doctors only realised how underpaid they were some five years ago. The vocational drive is still important in some areas, but probably dominant in none.

The last few years have seen a series of government incomes policies. From 1966 to 1970/2, 1973 and 1974 and 1975/6 and 1977, they are more the rule and atmosphere rather than the exception. We shall deal with these in more detail further on in the book, but one point must be made at the outset. Most incomes policies leave the control of incomes to the basic-wage increase, but allow existing overtime, shift and productivity payments to be paid. By and large, the white-collar worker has fewer opportunities to increase his or her earnings above the basic salaries by such methods than have his manual colleagues. The 1977 New Earnings Survey showed that a manual worker's earnings are made up to 75 per cent basic and 25 per cent other, whilst a non-manual worker gets 94 per cent from basic and only 6 per cent from other earnings. Thus, during periods of incomes policy, the earnings of white-collar workers rise considerably less than those of manual workers. These averages, of course, hide quite remarkable ranges in both money earnings and differentials (indeed negative differentials) but even so only underline an important part of the story.

Over the past five years there has been a very high rate of inflation. This has meant that more people are concerned with their take-home pay, their disposable earnings and what this will actually buy; their real disposable earnings. This means after deducting tax and national insurance contributions. More and more people have found themselves being able to purchase less and less. This has been due to incomes policies, to the poverty trap for the lower paid and the higher tax rates for the slightly better off. In purchasing terms it is clear that the middle-income groups have fared comparatively badly. Not unnaturally, the combination of being held back whilst others were not and being on the wrong end of deductions had a salutary effect on the concept of 'Well, I'm all right bargaining for myself.' They weren't; and some specialists, like computer programmers, defended their living standards by regularly changing their jobs.

The combination of progressive immiseration (especially as the middle classes tend to have a high percentage of fixed financial commitments) and the various insecurities must have been an overall stimulus to seeking outside help. The complexity of modern legislation and the inability of the individual to cope with it is yet another. Within this, various groups and industries are affected differentially and thus unionise more or less readily. There is little of conscious political decision in this whirlpool, merely a recognition that if there is a chance of getting better short-term benefits and increased security then, as management is no longer approachable by individuals, the union professionals must be used.

There is a strange corollary to all this. It may well be that those who unionised first have done the worst. Certainly those like the railway and mining white-collar staffs who unionised in response to their conditions many years ago have seen their industries dwindle. But equally, it is true that employers, generally wary with new unions, tend to be compliant for a limited period following recognition, and are more ready to accommodate the union's claims. This in turn stimulates fresh growth, based on the results of the bargaining.

Within the white-collar union sector there is great scope for increased membership. The private sector has by far the furthest to go. The finance industries, the city and company head office are only starting to become organised. Computer staffs and technical staffs are still both increasing in numbers. New industries and new processes bring change and these changes will stimulate union growth and emulation. In the public sector, local and central government unions have made far deeper inroads. Yet we still have entire non-unionised sectors such as the armed forces, although in the light of European experiences this state of affairs may not last long. If the DoE manpower projections are correct, middle-class unionisation will be as dominant in the next two decades as it was emergent in the previous two. One extra reason for this will be that, of necessity, recruitment into the new white-collar areas will be from amongst people whose family background embraced trade union-ism. In the same way, those who are members of white-collar unions today will bring up families familiar with trade unions, thus white-collar unionism is here to stay. As the problems confronting the members become more complex, so their needs will become more urgent and sophisticated. This is the challenge.

Chapter 3

Organisation and recruitment problems of white-collar unions

'Ye are brothers! ye are men!' – Thomas Campbell

The first distinction to be drawn in defining trade unions is between those affiliated to the TUC and those outside it. Then there are public-sector and private-sector unions and some which are a combination of the two. There are single-industry unions, restricted-skill unions and general unions. Some are sections of manual unions, some cater exclusively for specific or slightly more generalised professional members only. There are traditionally militant unions and those which (oddly) are traditionally weak; some are financially well off, others marginally exist. Some call themselves unions but are not, others are called unions but deny that they are. All claim to be free and independent but some obviously are not. To understand white-collar unions in total, we must look at some of the sub-divisions at more depth.

Within the TUC there are now thirty-six unions catering almost exclusively for white-collar membership. The membership has increased because of the return to the fold of some of the unions which were suspended and then ejected after registering under the Industrial Relations Act, 1971. There are another thirty-six unions which have some degree or another of white-collar membership. Outside the TUC there are over 340 organisations which, by virtue of their being on the list of trade unions, claim to be unions, although the bona fides of many of them are challenged by their TUC competitors. Many of these were automatically transferred from the 1971 Act register when the new provisions of the Trade Union and Labour Relations Act, 1974 became operative. Of these only just over one hundred have received certificates of independence although only 120 have even bothered to apply. We shall examine some of these at greater length later in the chapter, but in all they account for roughly another 500,000 members.

Two points should be made about this group. The first is that it is unlikely that the Certification Officer established under the Employment Protection Act, to certify unions as independent of employers and viable as free-standing organisations, could in equity grant many of them a certificate of independence. Second, of the largish bona fide unions outside the TUC, at the passing of the Employment Protection Act, nearly all sought affiliation in 1976 and 1977.

Why be under the TUC umbrella at all? The TUC is the national centre of British trade unionism, buttressed by the Scottish Trades Union Congress, which can have minor affiliations of purely Scottish-based unions as well. The Wales Trade Union Council is a part of the TUC. This is enviable compared with the numbers of antagonistic national centres in other European countries. It is the body which liaises with governments and the Civil Service, national agencies and employers in both day-to-day and policy-making matters. To be outside this ambit is to lose the ability to influence the formation of policies which affect the members of all trade unions and often all their relatives as well. To be outside is also a tacit denial of the precept that trade union members, whether managers or floor-sweepers, are employees, subject to capricious and arbitrary policies, capable of being fired and unable to set their own salaries or conditions of service unless a strong bargaining agent exists. Finally, the TUC has a series of principles, laid down at the Bridlington and Croydon Conferences, which control the movement of members between rival unions and which are adhered to quite strictly. A union outside the TUC has no such protection. It is this mechanism which has played such a large part in reducing inter-union conflict and kept the possibility of resulting industrial disputes to a minimum. It could be argued that a piratical union would fare far better outside the TUC, unencumbered by recruiting restrictions: this is extremely doubtful owing to the hostility that would be engendered by such anti-social behaviour. But in a larger sense of remaining part of the trade union movement, for both the reasons advanced above and also the co-operation of both the TUC and other trade unions in time of need (for example industrial disputes) it is vital to remain a member.

The next distinction is between the private- and public-sector unions, although this is not as straightforward as it might sound. The Civil Service unions present no problem except that they are not in some non-Crown Civil Service establishments such as the National Museums. NALGO is clear enough, too, with town hall staffs and members at the gas and electricity boards, and in transport and the NHS. Unions such as ASTMS, however, have members in both sectors, as do TASS and APEX, albeit not to the same degree. ASTMS has university, Health Service and nationalised industries membership along with quasi-public bodies, whilst APEX, TASS, MATSA all have nationalised-industry membership. The distinction means a great deal in bargaining terms.

Not all white-collar staff join white-collar unions, even if they decide to join a union at all. Interestingly enough, the non-industrial Civil Service unions call themselves 'black jacket' rather than white collar, a significant if somewhat esoteric difference. In both the public and private sectors there are white-collar members in basically manual-worker unions and generally a separate section for those members. The T&GWU formed its clerical section (ACTSS) as long ago as 1924 but MATSA, the rival NUGMW organisation, is far more recent. Other unions such as the EEPTU, AUEW and UCATT have separate sections for supervisory staffs, while yet others like NUPE and COHSE have a substantial minority white-collar membership in the NHS. One major reason for the formation of these special sections was the difficulty encountered as to which was the appropriate union when a worker was promoted. Even with the TUC procedures this is still occasionally a sore point in inter-union relations.

It is very likely that the membership of these sections will be limited in the long run, despite attempts by some manual unions, notably in the engineering industry, to retain promoted members. The first of the reasons is technological change. The main areas of promotion for a shop-floor worker are through the supervisory grades, usually as a charge-hand, foreman and supervisory upwards. As technology changes the production patterns and computer controlled or numerically controlled machines and tracks take over the bulk of industry, so the skills and expertise needed to supervise the operations will change.

It is unlikely that the shop-floor worker will have had the basic education or the technical skills to enable him or her to perform the job without a training programme. Supervisory roles will, as time passes, inevitably be less about management and skills and become more technically oriented. In all probability these posts will be filled from outside, probably by people with qualifications, often university degrees, who (as in Sweden and the USA) see the supervisory jobs just as the lowest rung on the management progression ladder, rather than as an end in themselves. This change has already started in some companies, indeed one of them in a Monopolies Commission hearing gave it as the main reason why they made higher profits than their major competitor. The change should not be underestimated, nor should its longer term social effects be ignored. To cut the shop-floor workers off from their only real avenue of promotion is to create cul-de-sac situations and the social repercussions could be very far reaching.

The second, self-limiting reason is status. Although there must be a tacit recognition by people joining any union that there is a fundamental identity of interest between all employees, when a pollster asks an average bank employee or local government union member for an opinion of trade unions in general, this might well be critical although some might defend their own union. Manual-worker unions allegedly are bodies which strike for no good reason, are ultra-left wing and are busily destroying differentials based on merit and hard work. Their own union activities are viewed differently. They would claim they take action only when it is absolutely justified and with due regard to professional standards and ethics. The fact that this view may not correspond to reality is neither here nor there: it is believed. To join a manual-workers' union is either to give away the status in the work-place, or to reduce status overall and, in so many cases, status is all that these employees have left to them. These media-oriented views are changing relatively quickly but they still exist.

An adjunct to this is the differentials issue. Most of the manual-worker unions will bargain for a closing of differentials, whether using a national flat rate interest (£6 per week) policy, or at the workplace in direct negotiations. This is understandable, but there are important and honest differences here. The white-collar worker has not always been tenderly treated in this market place and there is a reluctance to join unions with a negotiating programme which ends up squeezing differentials, even if the social logic is there. Some unions have voted to become parts of larger manual-worker unions. Their subsequent growth as compared with other separate and independent white-collar unions is low, despite the fact that they all seem to have widened their eligibility for membership as part of the process. Strangely, some large and effective manual unions have failed to make many advances in a period of rapid white-collar union growth despite the fact that they deploy considerable bargaining expertise for employees where they are the dominant union on the shop floor side. Until such times as the social consciousness of employees is raised to an astonishing degree, this psychological status barrier will remain.

Another (not inconsiderable) point is the complexity of need. The white-collar employee has, by and large, very different problems and remuneration systems when compared with his manual colleague. The suspicion amongst these employees is that a manual union, although it has undoubted expertise, has an unsuitable strategic approach for their needs. This may well be correct. The remuneration package concept is not widely held amongst manual-union negotiators and occupational pension bargaining has not been widely pursued. There are also the complex productivity and job evaluations so necessary in non-productivity areas which are often based upon entirely different traditions. For all these reasons it is most unlikely that the white-collar sections of most manual-worker unions will expand at anything approaching the rate of white-collar unionism in total.

The next sub-division is that of trade grouping, industry grouping and skill grouping. Some unions are based on a single industry, although even this statement must be treated with some caution. The TSSA has membership in London Transport, the docks and waterways as well as in British Rail; NALGO (the local government union) has members in the electricity and gas industries and the NHS. The Colliery Managers, the Steel Managers and the Post Office Engineers however, are all single-industry, single-employer unions. The Civil Service unions are in an odder position. Although they have but one single national employer, if the Civil Service can be so described (and leaving out fringe, publicly-funded bodies) they can hardly be said to be a single industry. Each government department is large enough in itself to be called an industry and the unions tend nowadays, after a series of amalgamations, to have membership across departments. Even the single-employer precept can be challenged because as the government spreads its influence and takes a more active role in British life, so non-Crown Civil Service employment grows, such as the Manpower Commission and the ACAS. In the private sector, NUBE, the bank union, has attempted to penetrate into the building societies and the insurance industry and there are few single-industry unions left outside entertainment, journalism and broadcasting, and insurance agents.

This move to expand is far more accentuated amongst the white-collar unions than amongst their manual counterparts. Unions such as APEX, ASTMS and TASS, which in the early 1960s were predominantly engineering-based, have widened considerably, ASTMS far more than the other two. Indeed, ASTMS is probably the most broadly based general union in Britain today. Its membership covers engineering and metalworking of all descriptions: electronics, universities, health service, finance, computers, civil air transport, petrochemicals, shipping, all manufacturing, non-Crown Civil Service agencies, publishing and commercial travellers. Indeed, there is scarcely a facet of British employment life in which ASTMS does not have representation outside of the Crown Civil Service and local government (although there are a few small historical pockets of organisation).

The movement to expand the base came about for two reasons. One was the fact that a single-industry based union is vulnerable to a run-down of that industry and, rather like a company diversifying its products for safety reasons, so unions diversified. The second reason is more a function of white-collar employees themselves. Most, though not all, white-collar workers have skills and, more to the point, they are often portable skills. For example, clerical skills can be employed in any situation, as can computer skills and medical skills and most technical and scientific skills. British management at all levels is notable for its use of a person's talents rather than industrial background so that it is not unusual to find a manager going from a frozen food company to a steel company. White-collar workers also tend to be mobile in a geographical sense. If white-collar unions were single-industry based, the turnover in their junior membership would be extraordinarily high, both incoming and outgoing. It makes far more sense to keep members when they change jobs across industries. Of course not all jobs are this portable. At present supervisory grades tend to have skills specific to a company, let alone an industry, as do bank and insurance company staff. One of the major reasons for the high level of mobility, both inter-industry and demographic, is the promotion ladder.

This is a factor which, as we have seen with foremen, is not a problem shared by manual workers. Typically, a white-collar worker will not only have some form of skill or qualification, either of which would have needed time invested by that person, but salaries have tended to be on the low side for at least the first five years of working life. To get to the higher salaries, promotion is needed – not the automatic increment, but 'grade-hopping'. In any one company the chances are limited, hence the mobility in search of an upward movement. The need to do so is itself two-fold. The first is that the employee recognises that he or she has forgone income during the training period, had to endure five years of low pay thereafter, and consequently feels that there is a lot of catching up to be done. The second reason applies to fewer employees, and that is ambition for that power and responsibility which exists only in the upper echelons of management.

This brings us to the unions which have membership in specific skills or grades. When the white-collar unions started in the late nineteenth century they were formed on the prevailing union ethos which determined that they should be based on individual skills or even grades. Railway clerks, tax clerks, elementary-school teachers and later draughtsmen, foremen, insurance clerks, shop assistants – all had unions specifically for them. Although some widening took place earlier it was only in the post-war years that the number of job titles expanded in the non-manual sector and the unions responded to this by increasing their catchment area. Most unions will now accept members covering a whole range of grades and jobs. NALGO runs from top to bottom of the non-industrial local government staff, as NUBE seeks to for bank staff. ASTMS represents all grades at the Prudential Assurance Company from the manual support staff right up to just beneath board level. Both APEX and TASS have raised their sights from being purely clerical and draughtsmen's unions to including supervisors, computer staffs, professional engineers and administrative staffs. After a series of amalgamations the CPSA represents a large slice of those carrying middle level stresses in the Civil Service. Indeed amalgamations have played a large part in the expansion of the functional base of the white-collar union sector.

In the manual union sector this move to more general recruitment has taken the form of the expansion of the two large general workers unions after a series of mergers. In the white-collar sphere the only general union is ASTMS. As the T&GWU now has skilled, semi-skilled and unskilled employees in membership across a very wide range of industry, so ASTMS has the industrial range and an even wider skill range. From doctors (in the MPU section) to clerical staff, from professors (Nobel Prize winners) to MPs, from very senior management to security staff, the range could hardly be wider. There are obvious negotiating advantages in such a position even if it means that the professional negotiator has a nominally more arduous task. Experience in one group can be transplanted into another. Sympathetic action, rarely if ever needed, is always readily available. New ideas from one group can be applied to others. The general, white-collar employees union is almost certainly the one of the future, provided that the union has expertise, knows how to use that expertise and is seen to be using it, backed by qualified central support services and a large central fund.

There is however a rearguard action being fought by people who believe, no doubt genuinely, that professional groupings' interests can only be represented by professional people. One problem is that these people, however well intentioned, are being used by others both to resist new union recruitment and to damage the existing unions, for reasons entirely unconnected with the welfare of the employees in question. These bodies came into prominence during the Industrial Relations Act era when they took advantage of the new and strange definitions of an independent union and became registered. At this time we had the strange spectacle of most 'registered unions' being basically anti-union and almost all unions unable to call themselves anything but 'organisations of workers'. An even stranger spectacle was the Health administration sitting down to talk with the TUC which was then a body which did not contain a single organisation legally capable of calling itself a union! The bodies that registered fell into three distinct groups: the professionally based quasi-unions, staff associations and those on the special register. These last were bodies basically professionally oriented (like the BMA), whose structure, or indeed charter, apparently would not allow them to become trade unions. They thus registered as non-unions on a register of unions! Some of them, however, under the pressure of competition have sought certification under the Employment Protection Act, 1975.

In the first group were bodies such as the UKAPE and the APST. Both bodies had restrictions which allowed only certain grades into membership, these grades being based on either qualifications or external institute membership. Both tried to get recognition using Section 45 of the Industrial Relations Act, 1971; both failed. The concept is still alive, although the organisations concerned operate at a low level of activity and have made very little progress. The Council of Engineering Institutes brought out a report in January 1976 which recommended that professional engineers should join a trade union, recommended the two organisations above, ignored established unions in the field such as ASTMS and TASS and settled on a small public-sector union, the EPEA. The report was a poor one, badly researched and informed, subjective and written without any consultation with the major, established unions and whilst the recommendation of the EPEA might seem at least a move in the direction of the TUC it also seemed and has proved to be impractical in spite of the EPEA's desire to expand. This is because existing TUC affiliates are in all the fields concerned and the no poaching rules will apply. At the time of writing this has become a live, though unresolved, issue with the EPEA (now EMA) taking the TUC to the High Court.

The appeal of the quasi-unions is unashamedly elitist. They allege that professional standards, which must be maintained, will be eroded by classic trades unionism, which may be their shorthand for saying no disputes at any time will be the maxim. Along with this they claim that professional people have certain problems which are unique to them. Both arguments are gravely flawed and do the professional engineers a disservice. First, they deliberately confuse the functions of a professional institute with those of a trade union, both of which can co-exist quite happily, as they have different tasks. Second, they ignore the industrial realities in that, in an employment situation, there are few if any special professional provisions, a situation compounded by the fact that the 'profession' does not really exist in the same sense as medicine or dentistry. It is ironic that this state of affairs exists because of the internecine warfare between the different engineering institutes; the very people who preach the 'profession' versus the union. At the time of writing the quasi-union organisations have a minuscule membership and little appeal. After all, people join a trade union to have it bargain on their behalf. Not only have these organisations no experience of this, but they lack the funds to buy in any necessary consultation or establish the infra-structure to aid them. Finally, people are not so naïve as not to recognise that by forswearing industrial action the major bargaining card has been given away before negotiations even start. It need never be used, but it must be there.

The second group is comprised of run-of-the-mill staff associations. The majority of these are management-inspired, management-aided, management-funded and thus management-controlled. The overwhelming reason for staff association formation is to keep out a genuine trade union and hence management's interest. There have been occasions when a ballot of membership was held to see if a union had sufficient membership for recognition, where a staff association has been given equal status on the ballot paper, even though it had no paying members but existed merely on a piece of paper with a company-provided secretary and chairman. Staff associations have been characterised by an extremely low or even non-existent subscription rate. This gives them a 'price' advantage over genuine unions and can be justified because the staff association generally has no independently paid full-time officials (they may be seconded by management) and most other costs (postage, printing, rent, clerical facilities, etc.) are paid for wholly by management or provided free. Furthermore as no serious bargaining is ever undertaken there is little need for money to pay for back-up services.

An employer can make a staff association look independent by arranging for a very long-term loan at very low interest rates from a body with whom it deals in business. As the association is based on a company and as those bargaining are also employees, they are at a severe disadvantage and the settlements obtained often reflect this. Why then do people still join them and not a union? Staff associations can generally use notice-boards and the internal post, unions cannot; staff association officers get time off, union lay officers could not, although this is changing with the Employment Protection Act and the 'Time-Off' Code of Practice. A recent case might explain. At the Guardian Royal Exchange Assurance Company, the management and the staff association literature attacked ASTMS officers, suggesting control by leftists and most importantly, stated that the staff association's negotiations had produced the highest settlements amongst insurance companies. This document was issued late and to every staff member and no time was left for a logically pointed refutation. The figures were wrong, the conclusions were wrong and the GRE staff, lagging behind to start with, were left even further behind.

These are typical tactics, but in the longer run they have always rebounded. Before long, the staff realise that they have been hood-winked and then when they join a union will be far more angry and militant. It has happened repeatedly in insurance and is duplicated elsewhere with precision.

The Certification Officer, in charge of determining which are the independent unions under the Employment Protection Act provisions, has an important role to play in the control of staff associations. The finance sector, which includes the old-established bank staff associations, has over the years shown more resistance to trade unions than any other. How many of these will be adjudged to be independent is any-one's guess, but certainly at the end of 1978 one would expect to see a significant reduction in the total number in existence.

The definition of independence in the Employment Protection Act does, however, leave much to be desired. As it stands it has no base in industrial relations, no notion of effectiveness and bears all the hallmarks of a section drafted by a civil servant to whom a staff association is more readily associated with the army. The government itself realised this by attempting to amend its own bill, albeit at the last moment, in the Lords, but the amendment was withdrawn by the Leader on the rather odd grounds of a 'a thin House'. Since then there have been four further attempts to change the definition, one by Lord Briginshaw, two by Stan Thorne MP (an ASTMS member) and one by James Lamond MP (a TASS member). All were defeated or withdrawn.

The problem is that the only people who can possibly benefit from the definition are staff associations and other quasi-unions. It is clear that TUC affiliates are independent (some people feel only too so) and thus a Certificate of Independence is gratuitous. However, the main charge made against staff associations is that they are not independent and certainly not effective. Yet although the definition in the Act will rule out the really bad cases the more sophisticated employer will arrange for the appropriate changes to be made. It is sad to report that such subterfuges have 'taken in' the Certification Officer.

He claims, however, with some (though not total) justification that the definitions plus two Employment Appeal Tribunal decisions have made his decisions inevitable. Whatever the reason, a Certificate, though of little importance in practical terms, acts as a sort of 'Seal of Good Housekeeping' approval. Despite TUC opposition, an opposition reflecting its composition, the authors both hope that the concept of 'independence' will ultimately be withdrawn. It is superfluous and it can only lead to poorer industrial relations in the long-term – whilst even the Commission on Industrial Relations under the 1971 Act took effectiveness into account when looking at quasi-unions. If the law remains as it does at present, imposing on industrial relations without either understanding or taking part in them, the probability of at least one serious and nationally damaging dispute merely as a result of its existence, is very high.

Many white-collar unions, notably NUBE, ASTMS and TASS, have lodged objection after objection to the issuing of Certificates to staff associations and other quasi-unions. A majority of these failed and those that succeeded are failing on second applications. Given the high feelings engendered and the history of the cases the explosion we have just referred to is justified in trade union terms.

The final grouping is of the non-union unions. These are not important in this examination. The BMA altered its rules recently to let it act legitimately as a trade union, something it had been doing for many years in any event. Its virtual monopoly in the representation of doctors is now being challenged by some consultants and junior hospital doctors.

Others, such as the Royal College of Nursing, are not really unions and act more as professional associations, which indeed they are, although they play an increasingly challenged role in the NHS negotiating machinery. Neither of these bodies has stopped MPU-ASTMS, NUPE or COHSE recruiting and setting the pace for doctors and nurses. All the non-union unions are based on a single profession, but unlike the quasi-unions they are bodies with a history and with traditional functions. Sooner or later they will have to drop either the bargaining or the professional function because the expertise needed is now getting to be so specialised that a dilution of resources is neither practicable nor desirable.

To co-ordinate the activities of all these non-TUC bodies a new body was formed – the Confederation of Employee Organisations. Although it aims to have research facilities, etc., its membership is very small, the income low and its chances of getting off the ground can be discounted. There is one good reason why this should be so. It is neither needed nor wanted: other organisations are busily working in the field. Yet another new body claiming to represent these interests on a national basis has recently been formed yet this too will prove to have an inadequate base, both in sheer numbers and in genuine representative status.

These three types of non-TUC unions have not always encountered unqualified management approval. The BMA is not the most popular body at the DHSS, but they prefer to deal with it rather than MPU-ASTMS. Bodies such as the BMA or BDA are not recognisable as trade unions; indeed, one of the authors was subjected to considerable abuse by a caller in a phone-in programme when he suggested that the BMA was a trade union. They combine the professional association with the union; it is interesting and instructive that the professional bodies in the legal, accountancy, actuarial and architectural professions stick to being professional bodies. They debate and form standards of conduct to lead and instruct in professional and technical matters – and so they should for they fulfil these functions admirably.

Professional bodies are no more trade unions, however, than are unions professional bodies. A listing as a trade union under the Trades Union and Labour Relations Act does not magically confer a negotiating skill (or the wherewithal to acquire it). Bargaining nowadays is a highly sophisticated skill needing large resources – something one suspects the Engineering Institutions hierarchies knew only too well when they made their aberrant recommendations. The professional-versus-union argument is a non-argument: the two are mutually compatible, not inconsistent.

The cry professional is often caused by a strange speech defect – the person meant to say political. Are standards amongst the top echelon of civil servants lower because they have affiliated their union, the First

Division Association, to the TUC? Are they professionally less competent? It is, however, a serious matter. For jobs such as engineers there is no one employer: engineers (or accountants, etc.), work in large and small companies, across industries and sectors. His or her salary is set by those of the groups above and below in the hierarchy and those groups the company adjudge to be peer groups. To suggest (as the CEI suggested) that a small union, albeit skilled in national bargaining, could handle this sort of local problem showed a lack of knowledge of industrial relations that was frightening; or a substantial insight, an even more frightening thought. What is even more amusing is that the employers, by and large, do not want yet another union in, they only fragment bargaining and ferment trouble. The CEI got it wrong from all directions.

It is not only the BMA and engineers of this world that create the problems. The smaller professional bodies, now legally independent unions, have an impact on NHS bargaining. What makes matters worse is that legitimate unions sometimes have the legitimate causes of the members held back by a body such as the Society of Remedial Gymnasts. The Whitley Council system allows this to happen.

ASTMS has a basic rule. Never, ever, get into joint bargaining arrangements with a staff association – to do so is to invite disaster. A staff association will ride on the legitimate union's coat-tails; will work to poach its members and will charge less to help it do so whilst both bodies have to work at the pace of the other. The union cannot win. Not all unions have taken this view.

The NUBE went into joint bargaining with the bank staff associations in national level bargaining. It does not, however, appear to have succeeded and in 1977 NUBE pulled out of the national bargaining machinery. The bank employees are now faced with national level bargaining with their staff associations – not a very daunting proposition – and company level bargaining from NUBE, both at the same time. As we said earlier, in the long run the staff association nearly always proves counter-productive to the employer who sponsored it in the first place.

These three types of bodies have one major inconsistency in common: they all preach the virtues of professionalism and they all profess to believe in the structured, calm approach. Yet they suspend their beliefs when it comes to trade unions themselves. The more professional a union, the more successful it is and the more unionisation it shows, the more vituperation it draws upon itself from these quasi-unions. It is clear that these motives are at least as political as they are industrial – and that the politics are employers' politics.

It is against this background of a large variety of competing TUC-affiliated unions and the obstructionism of employers manipulating many of the non-TUC bodies, that recruitment takes place. There is a very marked difference between recruitment of members in the white-collar and manual-worker areas.

On the manual-worker side, individual large companies are well organised and the same applies to the whole of the public sector. If closed shops do not exist then the prevailing ethos is for trade union membership and the union penetration is high. On the white-collar side that ethos either does not exist at all, or is much weaker. As a result recruitment is much more difficult. An added complication is in the size of the groups involved. If there are 100 shop-floor workers it is unlikely that there will be more than ten supervisors, thirty clerical, administrative or computer staff, and ten managers. Thus, in recruitment terms, there has to be much effort for a small membership increase.

Unions have very different approaches to this problem. NUBE employ junior recruiting officials to tour the banks, and other unions have specific officers with specific recruiting tasks or responsibilities. Other unions such as ASTMS take a more reactive approach and wait for potential members to come to them before setting a campaign in operation. Whatever method is chosen, it is often a virgin field where there is overt hostility, often irrationally political, from the management, which overlaps to the staff themselves. We have seen how managements will sponsor a staff association and then give it a 'sweetheart' procedure agreement to keep unions out, but other tactics can be used.

As a rule, management resigns itself to union representation for its manual workers – it is an expected state of life. The same managements, however, have often viewed their staff joining a union as a betrayal and have fought it with unprecedented malice. It is not viewed as a normal development because the staff are thought by senior management to be an extension of management itself, hence the extraordinary ill-will that can be generated and which has resembled family rows or even civil war. Most managements will tolerate a small percentage of their staff in a union but start to worry if the numbers begin to approach levels which would mean recognition of the union. At these times whole armouries of tricks have been brought into play. The first is the 'we don't need an outside body interfering in our cosy family' approach. Then there is the threat, often veiled with 'we have you marked for promotion, but if you join a union . . .' Quite remarkable numbers of employees are promised promotion when a recruitment drive is in progress. There has also been the more positive suggestion to a prominent union member who is seen leaving union literature around. This is generally in form of 'the company feels that you should be transferred, as a promotion, to our Falls Road, Belfast, branch'.

A white-collar employee will not join a trade union without a reason. We suggested some of these in broad terms in the previous chapter. Reduced differentials, redundancies, increasing size of the organisation, government income policies and the effect of inflation on purchasing are often the recruiting sergeants. There are myriads of supporting stimuli each depending on the conditions in the place of work and the relationships there. Arbitrary decision making with poor communications, imposition of new work methods, the arrival of a management consultancy team, an impending take-over, poor work environment, are all reasons for joining a union. Others have included a predominance of women staff and unequal pay and opportunities, the arrival of a computer, and the realisation that friends in unions are getting larger increases. This last factor is not as self-evident as it may sound. Many employers, especially the smaller ones, do not publish their pay scales and in any event run secret merit-bonus schemes. The employee thus has the greatest of difficulty in finding our whether or not he or she is doing well in relation to the internal pay situation. Externally, there is an extreme reluctance, even amongst close friends, to discuss salaries in detail and the major source of information comes from advertisements for jobs, chance remarks, newspaper reportage or from an officer of a trade union. It is quite usual that even when employees have joined a union and have gained recognition, the first claim on their behalf leaves them amazed when it is demonstrated how badly paid they are in relation to others doing similar jobs.

How, then, do these employees join a union? Quite often a small group of members approach the union head office and an official is sent to discuss the situation with them and will probably set up a meeting in a local venue. Sometimes a member takes a job in a small company which is not unionised and starts to recruit; rather as a seed transferred on the wind can germinate on previously barren ground. In the case of the multi-plant companies, the recruitment tactics will be dictated by their internal structure. If it is centralised then recruitment will take place on a company-wide basis; if decentralised then on a divisional or site basis depending on where the responsibility rests for setting wage levels. A national recruitment campaign obviously requires considerable organisation and co-ordination and to this extent the larger the union and its resources, the greater its chances of success.

The first thing is to make people realise that the union exists. The next is to establish that it is a suitable union and then to overcome the residual prejudices against trade union membership.

Although most employees have heard of individual union leaders, the unions themselves often remain a mystery. ASTMS probably gets more publicity in the press, and on radio and television, than most other unions, both locally and nationally, but identification has had to be pursued purposefully. Some of this has been as a result of conscious endeavour, some has naturally come out of the work that the union normally undertakes but, whatever the reason, it is of inestimable advantage in recruitment work.

It is, however, often necessary to leaflet an office or works, preferably with a specially prepared document aimed at the staff in question, naming the employer and concentrating on their problems. This can range from five supervisors, to 35,000 ICI staff, through to 2,000 NHS speech therapists – scattered all around the country. Meetings and literature are the basic local-level weapons. At national level, ASTMS has tried advertising in the press and on the railways, and at railway termini, as has the USDAW. This has been successful in further defining the union image. The white-collar sector is more about persuading non-trade unionists to join than poaching other unions' members.

The advertisement campaigns were most successful. The first full page in *The Times* in 1968 stated 'The board and I have decided we don't like the colour of your eyes'. It drew a remarkable response: the head office switchboard was jammed for days with queries, mainly from middle management. Others, such as 'My tragedy was I picked up a pen instead of a shovel', and 'I would rather be on the dole than join Clive Jenkins' also drew good responses. At least one of the advertisements was aimed at an individual employer, but the indirect spin-off from this type of advertisement must not be underestimated. ASTMS used Independent Television for a Tyne Tees campaign but failed to have one accepted about a ballot at Cambridge University, when Anglia TV were refused permission to screen it. At the same time, and far more sinisterly, a regional newspaper refused to accept an advertisement on unspecified grounds. Privately, the union was told that the company whose staff was the target had told the editor that if he printed our advertisement, they would withdraw all their advertising. In the event he didn't have to, and the company became organised anyway – but later in recruitment there has to be a measure of persuasive activity.

Employees will want to know what they will be getting for their subscription. Previous successes will be reported, the union's expertise will be placed in the forefront; services that are provided, such as legal, education and research are all well publicised. For white-collar staffs this is important, as indeed it should be, for no union will be able to function well over the long term without such back-up. In the last analysis employees will, if given the opportunity, join the union which gives them the greatest chance of success in negotiating, whether this be about redundancies, the remuneration package, or job evaluation.

However, recruitment drives are not always entirely successful. SLADE launched an ambitious drive to recruit advertising agency staffs. Whilst they may well have had a great deal of sympathy if they had confined themselves to their traditional recruiting area, they attempted to get all agency staff. Various sanctions were applied to several companies but to no avail and the ensuing ballots were disastrous for the union which had taken on a very difficult industry. The number of agency staff recruited was small overall while the general bad publicity and hostility generated set all unions back in a jungle-like industry. The case of IBM at Greenock was unhappy for the unions involved (including both ASTMS and TASS). An ACAS survey showed not only low membership, but also low interest in membership. The only crumbs of comfort that the authors have is that IBM is the exception to the computer industry rule and that ASTMS did come top in the survey.

Choices, admittedly, are nearly always made on imperfect information and union selection is no exception. The information can be presented by the union about itself, or it can be passed on either by word of mouth or in the media. In the latter cases the successes, the successful negotiations and the breakthroughs, tend to be passed on at conferences, between people in clubs and pubs, whilst the militancy is published through the media. Few people will pay subscriptions to a union that achieves little or nothing if they have a choice. Occasionally there is no choice – the TUC Bridlington arrangements restrict it – but then those members who are dissatisfied should work within their own union to bring it up to the level they demand. A union is only as good as its members, although the professional staff obviously can help shape members' attitudes.

One other method of recruitment is the union merger. This is not the type of merger between unions of roughly equal size, but the attraction of a smaller union by a larger one. Staff associations have now developed a habit of 'kicking over the traces' and merging with a union, especially when the members realise how badly they have been treated. Small organisations have increasingly found it impossible to cope with the exigencies of modern collective bargaining and their own servicing and cash-flow problems. They have neither the expertise nor the money to buy in the expertise. The trend is undoubtedly to the larger unit in the trade union movement and it is unlikely that there will be many, if any, unions of under 40,000 members a decade from now. At present there are twenty TUC-affiliated, white-collar unions in this category and very many more outside the TUC umbrella.

There is one final point about recruitment. It is unfashionable, indeed often illegal, to distinguish and certainly discriminate between men and women, yet in this instance it is necessary. There are over one million women members of TUC white-collar affiliates, yet there are about four million women engaged in white-collar work. The Sex Discrimination Act and the Equal Pay Act will, in all probability, reduce this number in the short term, especially as their implementation coincides with a depression, but they will also guarantee an increase in the longer term. In trade union terms women have always been difficult to recruit: 55 per cent of men as against 32 per cent of women are in unions. Traditional wisdom suggests that this is because of the hiatus marriage and childbearing causes and the consequent part-time and temporary employment that ensues. Yet nearly half of all women workers are in white-collar employment and recruitment of these women is vital if unions are not to be weakened by large pockets of non-unionised labour.

Some unions have a preponderance of women members. APEX has more women than men, as does the IRSF, the CPSA and the NUT. Some unions employ a 'women's officer', others prefer to treat all members as indistinguishable. From a recruitment point of view it is difficult to get to potential women members. Many cannot attend evening meetings because of domestic commitments (it will take a revolution in attitude, not legislation, for this to change) and often women are not as motivated by job security. Again, to date, the career has not been a high priority and all the available data would indicate that women, because of social malformations, have been more resistant to change in the workplace. These differences in approach will have to be met by unions, which have not been conspicuously successful at this in the past. It may be that the 1975 legislation will change this state of affairs, but what is certain is that entrenched attitudes will only change over some considerable time. The real problem is that any discrimination in recruiting literature itself is inappropriate and may even be illegal.

In the course of this chapter we have used the concept of a union providing expertise more than once. This is vital if the union is to do an adequate job for the members who fund it. We shall now look at white-collar unions, what members need and the leverage unions provide which the average member cannot personally deploy against an employer.

Chapter 4

The mechanisms of a white-collar union

'The tasks of working out salvation By mere mechanistic operation' –
Samuel Butler

At the beginning of the century and then for the twenty years following
the First World War, it was possible to conduct a negotiation swiftly
and with the minimum of fuss. For, at least half of the time, the unions
were fighting management proposals for wage cuts, rather than putting
in claims on their own behalf. Battles over wages and working conditions
were conducted on a remarkably unsophisticated basis: the lines were
drawn up over basic principles. Strikes were common and they were
long, painful, and miserable with owners trying to starve employees
back to work without re-employing the strike leaders. Despite the hard-
ships and despite the family distresses, remarkable victories were won.
These laid down the basis for the trade union movement of today.

Today the battle-lines are more indistinct. Negotiations are far more
complex as the regulations of conditions between employees and their
employers are affected by various laws, incomes policies and the complex benefits themselves. Outside the new problems with toxic materials,
it is rare to find negotiations directly about life and death as they were
at one time. Strikers, although they do not live well on it, have some
form of social security underpinning their own and their families'
existences. The relationship between capital and labour may not have
changed fundamentally over the years, but the conditions in which this
relationship exists have changed greatly. The white-collar union is the
inheritor of this tradition, yet although it adopts basically the same
tactics, it has to have, by virtue of its membership and the fields in
which it is working, many other tactics and ploys for offence and
defence.

The members and their attitudes tend to dictate the tactics and
policies of any union. In the white-collar sector, where there are so
many members new to unions and so much first generation bargaining,
this is especially important. The first thing to realise about the membership is the mobility which affects the turnover rate. For a union such as

ASTMS to increase its membership by 30,000 over a year generally entails recruiting over 70,000 and this is low by most general union standards. The reasons for members leaving any union are legion. Even dedicated trade unionists die; companies shut and members are made redundant; because the immediate danger surrounding their jobs which stimulated the membership has disappeared memberships lapse and members are expelled for non-payment of subscription. This has been true of the white-collar fields in particular. We have already touched on the mobility of white-collar employees; their new jobs may well take them into other unionised areas and they then have to transfer out to their new union. The turnover tends to be highest in unions with a predominance of women members and younger, unskilled staff workers.

A high turnover means that a premium is put on the collection of subscriptions. To provide any sort of service, money is needed, so that the cash-flow position of a union is important. As one would expect, the higher the income, the more services that can be provided is the rule. In the recent (high inflation) past many union subscriptions have not kept pace with inflation with a result that many such unions are worse off now than they were three years ago. ASTMS (at the centre) now control an inflow of around £5·7 million (1977) with £7 million expected in 1978, and even smaller unions such as APEX attract £1·8 million and TASS £2 million (both in 1977). Nearly all (if not all) of this will be used in current expenditure of various descriptions, salaries, postage, stationery, strike pay, and all the normal running costs associated with any enterprise in Britain.

Because of their age, and previous small size, few of the white-collar unions have a considerable investment income (the Transport Salaried Staffs Association being an exception), and this is an important difference between them and the manual workers' unions. The manual workers have built up their reserves over many years at quite a high membership level, as did the TSSA, but most of the other white-collar unions have had far less time to do so.

In addition many old-established manual workers' unions have substantial Friendly Society funds along with diminishing demands on them. The funds however tend to be 'locked in' and unusable in the generality of a trade union's work. Despite the short time-scale, there has been a period of rapid growth of membership. This needs money both to cover initial recruitment and because new members need more money spent on them in the early days; for meetings, on the first generation negotiations, on education and on general detailed counselling. The public sector unions are better off (and NALGO is relatively affluent) in comparison with their private sector counterparts. The big unions own property; others have leases, some rent, but in general this property ownership is small. At least one union owning a considerable amount of property has run into minor liquidity difficulties.

The liquidity position, as opposed to assets held, is very important for a trade union. Although it is possible to budget for normal running costs over the coming year, if the rate of inflation is correctly computed, it is usually impossible to predict what dispute pay will be needed. A union can never afford to be put into a position where it cannot fund a dispute, although, of course, many forms of industrial action need no funding. Once employers realise that a union is in financial straits they also realise that one of the main bargaining weapons has been removed and consequently negotiations become much more difficult. Although, of course, it is possible to get loans against assets held, this can often take time and the time scale is of vital importance when a dispute comes to a head; hence it is preferable to keep a certain proportion of assets as liquid as possible. A union with a few hundred thousand members will always have a considerable monthly income and it is now becoming necessary for such unions to place this money in the short-term market or in deposit accounts to maximise its income, or at least minimise the ravages of inflation.

Oddly enough, the subscriptions paid by members in the white-collar sector are not high in comparison with many manual unions, despite in many cases offering a wider range of services. Not only is the range wider but it has to be spread over a greater number of negotiating groups, each of which has, in comparison with manual unions, few members. This is basically a private sector problem and results from the multitude of domestic negotiations as opposed to the public sector's national-level bargaining. In some cases, this can be as small as half-a-dozen persons. From a cost effectiveness point of view this is absurd but also important, for a union must not have first- or second-class members and so must, if the need is there, service a group of six as thoroughly as a group of 600. Unfortunately, the time taken, the man-power used and money expended is often the same in both cases, perhaps even more in the case of the small group. This militates against a strict definition of cost-effectiveness and makes for a more arduous life for white-collar trade union officials.

One method of coming to terms with this problem is education. If a union can train its lay members to undertake normal bargaining competently, then the strain on the professional resources is diminished. There are, of course, other very good reasons for wanting to provide education in labour relations matters, both philosophical and practical, but the negotiating task is a most important one. The TUC and educational bodies work in this field but the effort is insufficient, more specific member-union oriented courses are needed. Although most unions have an education officer, generally the level of activity is still inadequate. The TUC was singular in Western Europe in not having financial support from the state to help with its educational work. After considerable debate, however, the General Council raised the question with the government in Autumn 1975 and finally received a small annual grant of £650,000 in 1977, which was increased to approximately £1 million in 1978. Of this the lion's share goes to the TUC Educational Services and the remainder is distributed to affiliated unions, both those with their own schools and those who run external courses. The 1974/5/6/7 legislation intimately affects collective bargaining and virtually all relationships at the work place and members who have to negotiate will need to understand it, if adequate and purposeful use is to be made of it. We examine this legislation in more detail in Chapter 7 and elsewhere. Individual company economies are of vital importance, not just the reading and analysis of accounts, but also the future prospects of the enterprise, the investment record and its manpower planning. Historical perspectives and bargaining techniques must also be taught if the members are not to be placed at a disadvantage when confronting management. The aim must be to get at least one member in every group to hold their own in negotiations.

Union colleges are now assuming a key importance; the ASTMS college in Bishops Stortford can handle 1,800 students per year, on a one-week familiarisation course and a one-week advanced course basis. For a white-collar union this is a vitally important initial step. It is one thing to recruit members, it is quite another to retain them by providing the best possible service.

It must be remembered that so many members have little or no previous union experience and thus it becomes most important to teach techniques and the union movement ethos. If members can be provided with the basic negotiating skills the professional officers will be released to conduct the secondary negotiations and to negotiate the trend-setting agreements which benefit all the union members in the longer run. But these brief courses fall far short of the type of training necessary for the activists who will be seconded by their employers (under the Employment Protection Act's provisions) to work part time or full time for the union. Also they do not attack the question of educating employees to become the trade union members of company boards (as may be required by UK or EEC legislation for worker directors) or to play a full role in open industrial democracy institutions.

The Employment Protection Act gives all unions the right to information from employers so as to conduct collective bargaining adequately. Thus all unions will have a large educational problem in getting their active members to understand and qualitatively assess this information.

White-collar unions have a somewhat more complex problem: not only is the scope of bargaining greater, but the elements tend to be more complex. Job evaluation exercises are the norm, rather than the exception; pension fund negotiations are routine; the salary package with trade-offs between, say, car allowances or cash is a growing problem. All these factors have to be taught and taught thoroughly – once started on a negotiation a union representative cannot ask for it to be abandoned because he (or she) has come to the limit of his knowledge. This is why, to be successful, a white-collar union has a far greater need of educational resources than does its manual union couterparts.

Some unions, such as the NUT, place great stress on the educational function whilst NALGO have a department of twenty-five people dealing with this subject alone.

There is little in the white-collar union structure that distinguishes it from the manual union. Both have members grouped into branches, each with officials; these may be 'closed' (based on a single employer) or 'open' (based on many employers). Unions differ as to whether branches are then grouped into areas, divisions, or regions, but the underlying mechanism of an aggregation of branches into a larger unit, or perhaps a two-tier system of larger units, remains very similar. The turnover of members, as we have indicated, is extremely important. NALGO estimates 30 per cent of members move during a year and this makes a good records system vital. Some unions own and use a computer for record keeping, notably TASS and NALGO, some use computer bureaux whilst others do the whole process manually; this applies to both sections of the movement.

White-collar workers typically work in an environment where the written word is very much part of the work process. They are accustomed either to giving or to receiving instructions, being consulted and asking questions, and taking decisions in the light of information received. Although this cannot be said to apply to all non-manual workers by any means, it applies to a considerable percentage, and is in marked counter-distinction to the work operations encountered in the majority of the manual areas. We must hasten to add that this is not impressive as such, it does not imply any greater intelligence or ability; it does, however, have repercussions on the way white-collar unions have to operate.

The propensity to cope with and sometimes even to revel in paperwork, plus the need to keep in touch with small groups and the need for the unions to weld previously non-unionised employees into a cohesive unit, leads immediately into communications problems. The white-collar union invariably provides more written material of various descriptions than its manual counterparts.

First, and most importantly on a *flagship basis*, there is the union journal. Most unions, even small ones, provide a paper of some description, even if it only consists of a few duplicated sheets. ASTMS publish a bi-monthly journal, plus *Medical World* for doctors and NHS members;

an engineering journal; a quarterly *Finance News*; a journal for post-graduate and under-graduate students – *Viva*, and *Selling Today*, for its commercial-traveller membership: six major newspaper or magazine-type productions. The *ASTMS Journal* is mailed to the home addresses of every member, although some unions prefer to distribute them through place of work and send bulk supplies to offices, plants, etc. The NUT issues three monthly journals, NALGO issues two regular journals to branches and TASS, APEX, IPCS, CPSA, and NUBE all produce professionally edited and informative papers. Many have been improved as a result of the demand made by a literate and interested membership.

This is, however, only the publicly visible tip of the iceberg. Advice on new legislation, or important legal decisions, surveys of salaries and conditions, or administrative changes, have to be reported to the members. This is generally done through the branch system. At ASTMS there has to be a weekly regular mailing to all of the 850 branches and, on occasion, a mailing to all of the 8,000 plus groups. The Transport Salaried Staffs Association has a regular mailing to all of its branches every other day and to its National Executive every day. Most of the other white-collar unions use a regular mailing system and again this is a service demanded by members and far more prevalent in the white-collar sphere than amongst manual workers' unions. In addition to this, however, there are the more specific information demands to be met. Reports of meetings, details of settlements, proposals for changes in conditions, all have to be meticulously and carefully drafted, printed and disseminated. Additionally, ASTMS found it necessary to provide a quarterly *Economic Review* to branches, the first of its kind prepared by any trade union; two other unions now produce an annual review. Excluding the five journals, the ASTMS print shop makes twenty million impressions annually.

Communications cannot be overlooked. A union that wants to give the maximum independence to its members in their negotiations, and at the same time exercise an overall policy and tactical control, has a duty to provide the maximum amount of information. As a result, a good union can be remarkably free of unofficial disputes, since these often occur as the result of a breakdown in communications between the union centre and its active periphery.

Members in the multi-plant, multi-product company or laboratory technicians working in small groups at sites all around the country need to be able to meet to compare notes and prepare group strategies. Trade unions have set up combines, committees or National Advisory Committees for this purpose, and of course, these need servicing too. The result is that the white-collar union generally carries with it a higher ratio of salaried staff to members than does the average manual union.

Back-up and services staff are also needed in greater measure. Many unions have some form of legal department and this varies from actually having lawyers on the permanent staff to having an internal department acting as a sieve before passing cases to the union's solicitors. The NUT have ten people, NALGO nine, ASTMS six. These are in addition to the specialist solicitors and barristers unions have to employ. All employees can suffer from industrial diseases or injuries, all can be victims of unfair dismissals and thus all unions must provide facilities to process claims or prosecutions. Almost all members can be arrested on a picket line, so all unions must be able to defend members too. In addition there are legal and government enquiries where members have to be defended. These are growing in number, especially in the Health Service.

Not all unions have research departments, but those in the white-collar sector generally do. These departments vary in size and scope. TASS, for example, employ a department of nine people, but use their computer for information retrieval, NALGO have nine, APEX have nine, CPSA have seven, ASTMS have twelve, whereas the NUT have fifteen in a combined education and research department. Almost without exception the researchers are highly qualified graduates, often with second or third degrees. The greater the diversity of membership the harder is the research department's task; the greater the number of new members the more important its functions become. Researchers in a general union envy the researchers in the single industry union where they might have only four basic negotiations per year – at ASTMS there are over 5,000.

White-collar unions have to maintain research departments because their members used to be, by and large, less ready and less inclined to take any form of action unless logically persuaded of the virtue of their case, and so in each year a number of major claims, well documented and well researched, are written up. They are not generally aimed at the employer because all too often they are not adequately read and often make an inadequate impact on what is a commercially entrenched position. The claim in the first instance is aimed at the membership. It is part of an educational process and will seek to show, by varying methods, comparisons of salaries and conditions, inflation, corporate profits and a host of other specific matters, that the employees are at least deserving of the increase that is being claimed. It is a sad but true fact that employers in Britain will only make concessions when they are forced to; their first and lasting basic reaction is to cost-minimise when it comes to remuneration consistent with maintaining staff levels if not quality. This means that an employer has to be persuaded that his staff will, if necessary, take industrial action. No one likes to strike. The loss of income is often severe, the enforced idleness demoralising. In the white-collar fields this dislike is reinforced by attitudes developed outside the trade union movement. Information about relative conditions is the one factor which may persuade members that industrial action is desirable, indeed inevitable, hence the need for a well-argued claim.

Research departments also differ in their duties. Some have a parliamentary and political function if the union is socially oriented, others take on the responsibility of health and safety or legal matters. Claims, of course, are not the only 'bread and butter' function. 'Charters' which are, in essence, overviews of the organisation in question, are regularly produced, especially where new negotiating rights are established. Speeches have to be written, recruitment literature prepared, arbitration cases of a detailed and technical nature drafted, MPs briefed, submissions to government departments written, professional officials' queries answered, briefings given to officials sitting on committees and boards, and so on. Some publish sophisticated salary surveys (TASS for example), others often produce well-argued cases against, say, public-sector cuts, or for an expansion or change in telecommunications expenditure. The variety of work undertaken is immense, the quality extremely high.

One matter that exercises trade union research departments is the preparing of cases for arbitration. Whilst this is by no means confined to the white-collar sector it is somewhat more prevalent than amongst manually oriented unions. Some white-collar unions regularly sign agreements with employers where the last stage is compulsory arbitration (NUBE for example). This could, uncharitably, be called a sign of weakness. Other unions become involved with arbitration either because industrial action is inappropriate or because it is unlikely that the members will undertake to see it through. Others end up in front of an arbiter at the conclusion of an inconclusive dispute action.

For whichever of these reasons, preparing and presenting an arbitration case is very different from writing and presenting a normal claim. The facts and dates must be totally above reproach – the arguments are aimed at persuading a disinterested third party not to 'reinforce the troops'. Checking, re-checking and then double-checking is the order of the day in these cases – a slip in calculation would not be a debating point, it would be a disaster.

As we shall see later in the book, all these research functions are growing in importance. Consequently there is not only a tendency to increase the number of researchers but there is an equal tendency, disturbing to some traditionalists, to recruit ever more highly qualified staff. For each research assistant job advertised there have been nearly 100 serious applications during the past three years, a time of high and rising unemployment. The unions now have probably as good a selection of graduate applicants as industry or commerce. Even so, some services have to be 'bought in'.

Commercial library services, accountancy specialists (especially for tricky current cost-accounting exercises) and pensions experts have all been used by white-collar unions. Fortunately, as we said earlier, most unions have members who can voluntarily aid both research departments and officials by using their undoubted skills and expertise.

White-collar unions tend to use the same system of representation as their manual colleagues, although they are given a different name. The shop steward becomes the group representative, the convener is titled the chief negotiator. There are joint union, staff committees parallel to traditional joint shop stewards committees. At the larger, and more enlightened, sites the chief negotiator (who is also generally the group chairman or secretary) will have an office and secretarial assistance provided by the management. Formal contracts for such a state of affairs exist including the payment of salary, although the representative is wholly employed on union business. One major difference, however, is in the position of the full-time professional officials.

The older craft and other non-general manual unions traditionally have elected their full-time officials from within the membership of the union. At the time this was essential since few outside individuals knew about or were sympathetic to a trade union culture. Equally, the democratic nature of the movement was reflected in this form of accountability; if the members did not like the results of negotiations they eventually removed the negotiator. Often the executive committees of this type of union were made up of full-time officials, with the chairman or general secretary acting as the chief negotiator. The election system still obtains in some unions even today, although there are now variations on the theme. Some have appointment first, confirmed by election subsequently; others have elections but for a working lifetime at the essential 'pleasure of the union'. Normally the white-collar sector is staffed predominantly by appointed officers. Certainly, the older unions still elect officials but these are in a very small minority. The appointments are made by the executive committee of the union which is a lay elected body. This system has great advantages. First, it widens the range from which officers can be selected, if the union itself does not have members of a sufficient experience who wish to take on the responsibility, then recruitment can be undertaken from outside. Second, and most important, it enables an adequate professional approach to be developed.

Current negotiations, whether with an employer directly or with government departments and agencies indirectly, have never been so complicated. A body of knowledge and skill has to be applied and that can only be built up over a long period. The members rightly demand the best representation possible, since to them the unions act in defence of their industrial interests in much the same way as a doctor looks after their health and a solicitor after their legal interests. If a professional officer was capable of being rejected in an election, a rejection which would often be on political rather than industrial grounds, there would not only be a damaging lack of continuity, there would be little incentive to acquire all the expertise necessary. A full-time official does not have a political or policy-making job; he or she carries out all the necessary duties after the policy-making body has laid down the policy guidelines. In all unions this body, the executive council, is elected. It seems strange, but for some reason most unions have an ultra-left minority which campaigns for both the policy-making body and the full-time officials to be elected. Employers would love this to happen for, if nothing else, their jobs would then be much easier in a short-term economic sense because the trade union would be so preoccupied by the electoral process and thus have less time for bargaining. But the long-term relationships could become soured.

In white-collar unions the full-time officials come in all shapes and sizes. It must be admitted at the outset that women activists, even in unions with a majority of female membership, are very underrepresented. This is unfortunately as much a function of male chauvinism as female non-involvement, although it must also be frankly stated that the exigencies of the job do militate against women with young children being employed – most professional officials are expected to be available any time of the day, seven days a week.

The background of the officials varies remarkably. Some may have degrees, others may have worked on the shop floor, some may come from within the union membership, others may have been officials with other unions. The workload also varies from union to union. In some it is relatively light with little recruitment work and a few central-ised negotiations, whilst in others negotiations are decentralised and officers have to work hard. The type and structure of the union dictates which system prevails. Some unions have specified officials specialising in certain industries, other unions prefer to have the 'all-rounder', which is sometimes a much harder task. In almost all, however, there will be national officials with national responsibilities for industries and companies. The officer coverage varies too: it has to be where the members are, and this of course means officers around the country, but the ratio of members to full-time officials is very high. NALGO have approximately 170; CPSA, 30; APEX, 60; ASTMS, 101; TASS, 45; TSSA, 20; NUT, 20; NUBE, 40. Quite clearly the private sector union with a different set of industries to deal with and a high proportion of domestic negotiations needs a larger full-time officer strength per member. To cope with this demand for officials, ASTMS have had to set up a Trainee Officer Scheme where suitable but inexperienced people can learn the arts. In addition, some unions have, with the passage of new legislation, commenced appointing specialists in the fields of health, safety and pensions.

The full-time official has to keep abreast of all the current developments and techniques, both in the field of legislation and in new managerial gambits. The range of subjects negotiated by a white-collar union tends to be larger than the manual union range. The remuneration package, containing as it does so many elements, is basically a white-collar phenomenon and if it is to be bargained successfully there has to be a considerable knowledge of each of the elements and their relationship to each other. Incomes policies imposed by governments have to be managed so as to obtain the maximum return, members have to be consulted with, paperwork kept up to date, and branch administration overseen. Expertise there must be, the union members rightly demand it, but it must be applied in what are often the most stress-laden of circumstances. This is very much the case in a white-collar union where an official has to argue a sophisticated case forcefully whilst, at the same time, stimulating and orchestrating possible industrial action amongst members for whom this is an alien tactic. This often gives rise to staffing problems because of the acute shortage of experienced, mature and pressure-resistant candidates for full-time office.

So a white-collar union has to tackle problems which other unions do not and we have noted the mechanisms which they use to cope with them. The members of these unions, however, are different from those in the manual unions in some significant respects. Their inexperience in union techniques and lack of a labour movement background is, of course, responsible for much of the increased expenditure and work involved in this sector but there are important offsetting advantages.

Many members have not only acquired skills and qualifications, but they have positions in organisations where information is available. Both of these advantages can be and are tapped by the unions. If, for example, the TUC asked for comments on developments in the computer industry, at least two unions could consult some very senior members in the industry about prospects, research and development and market future without infringing on commercial secrecy. This entry into the world of commercial and technical expertise is even more valuable when lobbying a government department on behalf of members. It enables sound, comprehensive and sensible cases to be assembled. Its implications for the trade union movement as a whole and the TUC are very great and we shall explore these at greater length later. Some unions use their senior membership to provide studies and papers of equal standing to academic work on the same subjects. In spite of the long-run underfinancing of the British trade union movement, the estimate must be that this theoretical capacity will continue to develop.

There are well-documented studies showing that the 'take-up' of health services and possible welfare benefits and legal services is highest amongst the middle class. This ability and willingness to use services offered is true in a union sense too. If legal, research, educational and counselling services are provided they will be used in great measure by the members; if they are not offered the members are articulate enough to force the union into providing them. But the standards have to be high. A white-collar employee will simply leave a union if it does not provide what it promises. This is still relatively easy in a sector where closed shops have not been favoured, although the growing density of membership will undoubtedly check such movements in the future. If a management uses sophisticated propaganda techniques the union is forced to counter them in kind. Not all the services are unique to the white-collar sector alone nor, indeed, are the problems all that different in essence, only in detail. For example, the multi-national company poses a threat to the security of employment of all workers and all unions face the same problems, with perhaps a special problem for research workers when laboratories are moved across national frontiers and, because of a low capital cost, this is a favourite manoeuvre. One method of combating multinational activities is to join a multinational union trade secretariat and the white-collar unions do this as readily as any others. These are part of the larger parcel of affiliations which white-collar unions may make. Some, though not all of them, are affiliated to the Labour Party on the basis of the voluntary political levy. However, most of the public sector and all of the Civil Service unions are not so affiliated. Since mid-1977 every significant, independent union has been affiliated to the TUC which makes it the most representative of all the Western trade union centres. But there are a multitude of other affiliations which unions feel they ought to make. There is a generalised private industry based white-collar international secretariat to which some British unions affiliate but it has yet to make a significant impact on the worth of the movement. The large international secretariats, such as those for chemical and transport workers, public sector employees and food and drink industries provide for white-collar representation although the metal workers are only just now coming to terms with this changing circumstance. To complicate the picture there are now Brussels-based committees or sub-organisations of the principal secretariats which relate to the EEC and its consultative committees for industries which work on the periphery of industrial relations.

The members of white-collar unions give them their individual character and flavour. The industries they work in dictate many of the publicly struck attitudes. The basis in all of them is that skill, responsibility and effort should be rewarded and that employers, no matter who they may be, cannot be permitted to exploit employees simply because they have achieved some considerable status in the organisation. The type of member, however, also determines tactics. The vocal and literate demands for success have to be met by the professional full-time officials. This entails the setting up of specialist back-up departments, the appointment of literate and numerate negotiating officials and the pioneering of new techniques, for example, in the fields of job evaluation or flexible working hours. The officials clearly have different demands made of them.

The growth of the white-collar union is the most dynamic and exciting influence in the TUC arena today. They are providing the movement with new ideas, new expertise, new techniques and new enthusiasm whilst the movement provides them with a solid and stable set of values and philosophies.

In Chapter 5 we shall take a look at some of the techniques, some of the gains, some of the disputes and the bargaining parameters involving white-collar unions. As the concentration of unions progresses through mergers and society changes under the impact of technological development and social demand, so we may well find that all unions, white-collar and manual, will seek to bargain for similar results and an equal status in the labour market.

Chapter 5

Significant gains, significant disputes, significant techniques

'Suit the action to the word, the word to the action' – Hamlet

The industrial relations world is not anarchistic; it is highly structured, formal and deeply influenced by its history. Procedures are based on a pre-determined agreement; the steps are normally faithfully adhered to and hierarchical priorities maintained. Of course, as contracts get broken so agreements get broken, and when they are, a dispute is never far away, but in these cases if one looks behind the façade there is almost always an extenuating circumstance. The formality is under-pinned by the procedure agreement. This stipulates the subjects that can be covered by collective bargaining and the stages through which they can be processed. It may be a short document covering just these points – it may be a major statement of intentions and duties covering lists of relevant departments and grades and delineating very precisely the management actions which are constrained by prior negotiation.

But a procedure agreement can be negotiated only after the union has been recognised by the employer. Without recognition there can be no formal negotiations. One theory of white-collar union growth is that it was occasioned by recognition in the public sector and restrained by lack of it in private enterprise. As we indicated, there is certainly a validity to this. It would, however, be more accurate to put it in its negative form which is that without recognition a union will wither away. Employees join a union for the service that unions can provide and paramount in this is the ability to represent the members' interests. This can be done only if recognition has been granted.

Recognition is not always for collective-bargaining purposes. A representation agreement can be signed with an employer, especially where there is a small membership; this can give the union the right to represent its case but this is often only for individual grievances. In such a situation the union, which is obviously in a weak position anyway, can expect little beyond a hearing. What a union needs, however, is recognition for bargaining purposes. In a large organisation there is little

71

contact between the industrial relations departments and the staff and only marginal contact between managers in general and those managed. In a small organisation the contacts are in physical existence. When a union recruits and perhaps takes action, the personal relationships built up through these contacts are put under very great strain. This is neither an argument against unionisation nor indeed against action: it simply states a fact of industrial relations life. But as personal contacts are naturally prized, the work of organisation in small companies is difficult.

The Grunwick dispute makes these points quite clearly and force-fully. The managing director obviously took the original APEX recruiting intentions as a personal blow, in much the same way as the managing director of Con Mech did at the time of the Industrial Relations Act, 1971. The successful opposition to union recognition, or indeed membership, by the company was thus both typical and, unfortunately, predictable. The inevitability of the union defeat in this instance was at least as much due to the character of the dispute as due to the characters, circumstances and tactics involved. It does not have the significance, however, for the trade union movement as a whole that some commentators would have us believe (nor for white-collar unions, given that APEX was the union involved). It may, however, be a tragedy for the workers involved in that strike. So many factors in this case are atypical; so much fringe political effort, both right and left, has been expended and so much right-wing political capital has been clumsily made, that other employers would be loath to be tarred with the Grunwick brush in the future. Certainly only small companies would be involved in this sort of activity if only for the reason that if Grunwick's had been large the strike and picket would have succeeded in stopping supplies.

At Grunwick the managing director used a basically Victorian tactic – dismissal; it is, however, by no means the only one at an employer's disposal when confronted with an organising union. When an employer wishes to refuse recognition he generally uses well-known and well-defined tactics. The first concern is to keep the number of union members as low as possible. This can be achieved by intimidation. If this fails then both overt and covert action is usually employed to ensure employees not only do not join but actually leave. Most of these actions are now effectively banned by the Employment Protection Act, but the employer who talks to staff and junior management about promotion and divided loyalties can have an anti-union effect. Union activists in a pre-recognition phase are easily harassed, transferred or promoted out of the area. At one time engineering employers used to promote the shop-steward to foreman to weaken shop-floor organisation, but since staff unions started to take them into membership this practice has slowed markedly. It took a brave man or woman to resist these tactics. Fortunately for the white-collar unions there are (and have been) many determined people in Britain.

The problem has been as follows: a union recruits membership in a company reaching (for example) 30 per cent of those eligible to join. It then approaches the company to get recognition. The company, which has been refusing the use of notice boards, declining to allow union officials on the premises and has been carrying on selective, work-oriented harassment, simply dismisses the proposition. The union is not strong enough to strike or to take adequately serious action. Time passes, the union cannot deliver the goods and so the membership is discouraged and gradually lapses. There are variations on this theme. A company might sponsor a staff association. A company might agree to recognition on a national basis if a majority can be proved on all the sites, knowing that this is not possible. Constituencies for ballots can be changed to suit the company and as the union is at this stage dependent on the co-operation of the management, this can pose almost insuperable difficulties.

It was expected that the recognition provisions in the Employment Protection Act would eliminate many of these practices and later in this book we shall look at these in more detail. However, as recognition is the key element it is generally not presented on a plate by the employers. In strike-statistic terms in the white-collar sector there have probably been as many working days lost over recognition claims as there have been over the various claims on conditions of service. When DATA (TASS as it now is) was attempting to get recognition from the Engineering Employers' Federation it had two abortive strikes before the major strike, in 1924, which finally settled the issue. The NUBE was not able to get national recognition until after it had had a dispute with the employers; the scene is littered with the debris of past disputes, both in the commercial and the manufacturing sectors.

Recognition disputes can be the most bitter and protracted of all. At C. A. Parsons, the TASS membership struck for six months in an attempt to get recognition and force out a quasi-union. At the end of this period nothing had been settled because the Industrial Relations Act's provisions allowed the quasi-union to use new procedures. A half-year's strike is perhaps an extreme case, but there have been literally hundreds of white-collar-employee strikes to obtain recognition. To be fair, there is another side, but this again is in public employment. NALGO managed to go through their first sixty years without a single official dispute, on recognition or otherwise. In the past the disputes over victimisation of union activists were associated with the fight to get bargaining rights. One person was dismissed in 1971 for the 'illegal use of the photocopier': this amounted to the copying of a one-page letter and it happened at a plant of one of Britain's largest textile manufacturers. A whole range and variety of trumped-up charges have been recorded and there are enough staff trade union martyrs to fill many pantheons. Although the unfair dismissal procedures have been extended to dismissal for reason of union activities this can be difficult to prove. If an employer is determined not to reinstate an employee, even if ordered to by the tribunal, the only penalty is a financial one. This is very small when compared with the overheads of the average-sized company and an employer may well calculate that it is a fair price to pay for thwarting a union. At any event, as the Grunwick case has clearly demonstrated, providing no discrimination is shown by reinstating some but not others – dismissals for going on strike (in recognition disputes or otherwise) are perfectly fair.

As well as individual cases, inter-union problems have loomed large in recognition disputes in the past. One incident affected ASTMS, APEX and the steel unions which has ultimately worked in favour of the manual-workers unions while, at the same time, stimulating a non-TUC affiliate to organise in the area. This unfortunate affair, which reversed the recommendation of an independent Court of Inquiry, is no precedent in the light of growing influence of the new unions.

When recognition is conceded, this is usually acknowledged in a written procedure agreement negotiated between the union and the management. Although it is rarely the subject for a dispute in itself the odd occasion does arise. An agreement was negotiated with Henry Wiggin of Hereford (a branch of the American-owned International Nickel Corporation). The agreement contained a clause which virtually allowed the management to take any steps it wished in work allocation. Although common in the US, it is rare in Britain. Despite repeated attempts to have it removed, the company refused and a strike which lasted for eight weeks followed. The offending clause was removed, thus conforming to British standards. The pickets planted a commemorative tree on the spot where they were stationed. The opposite to this form of clause are those surrounding the *status quo* clauses. These state that if a union objects to a new work procedure the existing system operates until such time as the matter has been settled. These clauses are as bitterly contested by managements as management prerogative clauses are by trade unions.

We have looked at procedure agreements and recognition and in so doing have often mentioned disputes without analysing what they are and the staff attitudes to them. Disputes are the suspension or alteration of normal working by employees. When a procedure agreement is in operation, dispute action is taken only when all other procedures have been exhausted. There are the cases of this not being so, but these are few and far between, especially amongst white-collar unions. Disputes can vary. At one end of the range is a total withdrawal of labour and these progress down in severity through partial withdrawals, limited-time withdrawals, sanctions on the working of overtime, working precisely to a rule book, non-co-operation, work-ins and sit-ins. There are boycotts, blackings, sympathetic actions and trans-national actions. There are also one-off actions concerned with product delivery or development.

It has always been assumed that white-collar staffs and professionals will not take dispute action. Employers have assumed this and found it painfully otherwise: doctors showed that by banning overtime, money could be found which seemed impossibly lost when arguing rationally; civil servants have actually struck as well as operating sanctions on overtime; local government employees have struck over London allowances; radiographers, laboratory technicians, teachers, museums and broadcasting staffs have all taken action over the last three years in the public sector alone. The CPSA air traffic assistants, dispute in 1977 also showed that white-collar members have sticking power as well as the fibre to take the action. There have also been hundreds of disputes in the private sector. The national public sector disputes are well known as they attract publicity. The private sector domestic disputes attract only local comment and these are worth looking at in more detail.

The following data are taken from the Engineering Employers' Federation annual report, 1976/7. It thus understates the magnitude of the problem because not all strikes are reported and not all engineering firms are members of the EEF. In 1964 there were 19 strikes involving staff workers and 24,000 days lost. In 1972 there were 101 strikes and 210,000 days lost. In 1973 there were 133 strikes and 155,005 days lost, and in 1974 there were 163 strikes and 355,513 days lost. By 1974 this had increased to the level where 42,947 staff were involved – an average of 8·3 days per worker involved; 1975 and 1976, understandably, showed a fall in the number of disputes as the 'voluntary' incomes policy bit deep. In 1975 there were 131 strikes and in 1976 there were 82 strikes. The last decade has obviously seen a very marked increase in industrial disputes. It is interesting to compare these figures with those for manual workers over the same period. There were, as might be expected, given the far larger number of workers, far more strikes. In 1964 there were 238; in 1972 there were 1,082; in 1973 there were 1,102 and in 1974 there were 890, and in the same way the numbers fell in 1975 to 766 and in 1976 to 639; yet in all six years, indeed in nine of the last ten years, the average number of days lost in staff strikes was higher.

The same survey shows that of the reasons for staff strikes in 1975, wages and earnings accounted for 72·7 per cent of the total whilst the next most significant was the 7·8 per cent accounted for by trade union questions – generally recognition problems. For manual workers only 48·4 per cent of strikes were caused directly by wages and earnings problems. It is always only too easy to fall into the trap of interpreting data rigidly and drawing inescapable truths and we shall attempt to steer clear of this trap. However, even in 1976, 69·2 per cent of staff strikes were concerned with the salary package, as compared with 40·8 per cent of manual-workers' strikes.

Within the last decade, strikes (as distinct from other forms of industrial action) have increased by 850 per cent in the white-collar areas of federated engineering companies. An inspection would suggest an equally large increase in the other private sectors. Again, in Britain, it is apparent that white-collar militancy is on the increase in the public sector, too. It must be remembered that for every strike there are at least two other incidents of industrial action short of a strike. We have noted earlier in this book that both in real, disposable-income terms and in terms of differentials between manual and non-manual employees, the white collars are losing ground. It is equally apparent that at least in 1975/6, strikes over money were more common amongst white-collar workers than amongst their manual colleagues.

This juxtaposition suggests two things. First, if the causes of white-collar union membership growth are indeed economic rather than social and political, then it follows that those who had already joined would, if subject to the same economic pressures, become more militant. The second is incomes policy. 1973 was a year of continuous incomes policy with Phases II and III culminating in the miners' dispute. 1974, on the other hand, was a year basically free of restrictions and in that year it is obvious that, in engineering at least, the white-collar sections felt impelled to apply more pressure than the manual workers. As in the previous year there were ostensibly equal increases for both sectors, it suggests that in reality the white-collar section felt a need to catch up. The data suggest that this need acquired more urgency during 1975 and 1976.

Another interesting fact about the strike pattern is the number of days lost per striking employee – these can be a measure of the effectiveness of the direction of the strike. In academic parlance, a dispute may be either high or low profile. High profile is the situation where a dispute has maximum dislocation outside the immediate area of the dispute in the minimum of time. Low-profile activity is precisely the opposite. Coal miners and computer staffs and direct production workers would thus tend to be high profile; office and managerial staffs low profile. These are not precise definitions and one can certainly prove them wrong in specific instances – for example, switchboard operators in a commercial enterprise and many types of indirect production workers can be high profile. Equally, a high profile situation can, because of external circumstances, turn out to be low profile – for example, a stoppage of production staff at a car plant where there is a large stockpile of cars and a background of shortfall in demand. The average time taken to settle a strike is longer for white-collar workers and tends to reflect their relatively low profile. Thus, in 1976 the average time lost per worker in staff strikes was 12 days, whilst for manual workers it was only 5·3 days.

White-collar unions are more realistic about their own strengths and weaknesses than any of their observers. If there is to be a dispute it is in everyone's interests that it be short. The members want a settlement because it minimises loss of income; the employer because it minimises loss of business; the union because it minimises the amount of strike pay. For some white-collar unions, the position needs careful scrutinising. TASS, for example, has a membership which works predominantly in drawing offices. The work done in such an indirect department is not generally missed for a considerable time, as much of it is concerned with forward developments. The result of this very low profile is that TASS members often have to dig in for a long period. On the other hand, many ASTMS members are very high profile. Computer staff, without whom there is generally no payroll, foremen (providing the shop-floor workers agree to 'black' their work while they are away), doctors and medical personnel are all high profile. Local authority white-collar workers tend not to be, although some civil servants (notably in Employment Exchanges) are high profile. Most unions have a mix, but some are more advantageously placed than others when it comes to contemplating industrial action.

Employers have had a preconceived notion over the years that white-collar employees will not take action and have, therefore, pitched their offers at a low initial level. They have also calculated the amount of time needed for a strike to have an effect and have reckoned upon a return to work before the critical point arrives. This is one reason why some white-collar workers now have rotating strikes with one department involved for two days, another for the following two days and so on, enabling maximum pressure at minimum inconvenience to the members. In the same category come overtime bans and non-cooperation actions, both of which can be remarkably effective; but it must be noted that the majority of strikes are settled in less than one week.

Most TUC affiliates have a rule-book provision to pay dispute-pay to members out on official strike. Most of the non-TUC quasi-unions or staff associations not only have no such provision, but may well have a no-dispute rule. It is usually not necessary to take action, but it is essential that the employer should estimate that the members could and would do so. In truth the concept of strike pay is anachronistic. The weekly amounts are low when compared with earnings and married men's families receive supplementary benefits as well as tax rebates. Both single and divorced, separated or widowed women with dependants can claim for any dependent children in the event of a strike. The benefits are usually offset against strike pay and thus this represents a transfer of resources from the union to the state. The presence, or otherwise, of strike pay is a stronger determining factor in white-collar disputes because, usually, it is larger than in the manual union sector.

In the past two years there has been a concerted attempt to get employers to fulfil their obligations under the Equal Pay Act which came into operation in December 1975. One union, APEX (which has a majority of women members), ran several large disputes on this matter. There is no doubt that neither equal pay nor equal opportunities are afforded to women in employment in Britain. One has only to examine the clearing banks workforce to see that women make up the bulk of the lowest two grades and are also on the lowest pay rates. In the white-collar field, especially in the larger companies or organisations, the problem of equal pay in itself has largely been overcome. Difficulties tend to arise, for example, in the payment of filing clerks, generally women, *vis-à-vis* the payment of wages clerks, often men. Strictly speaking, one can argue that they are jobs of equal value; the problem is that they are rarely valued as such. When one of the job titles has a predominance of men it still gets the higher value.

This then becomes a matter of job evaluation. Consultants and job evaluation experts are everywhere in the white-collar sector, partly as a result of disparately paid and graded staffs consequent upon mergers, and partly because the managements themselves do not have the expertise to settle matters. Each consultancy has a different system, otherwise they could not all exist but although they all claim to use differing job evaluation methods, when boiled down, they nearly all have the same basic characteristics. Job evaluations which may change existing hierarchies and upset traditional patterns are thus of great importance to staff.

Job evaluation is, when stripped of its jargon, merely a method of ranking jobs in a logical manner. It does so by selecting particular factors and these can literally involve any factor relating to the enterprise; broad ones such as responsibility, skill and stress, or specific ones such as speed of calculation, ability to meet people, etc. These factors then have points attributed to them, either overtly or in a hidden weighted form and the resulting scores are compared. Factors, points and weights can differ as can the methodology; bench mark jobs, selected sample evaluations; total job evaluations from managing director to a general office junior, vie with selected job-range evaluations with different factors for each range. One method at least, involving consensus, generally allows a union to interpose itself into the system as it relies on the staff themselves selecting the factors and weightings.

In the past, a job evaluation exercise was seen by the workforce as being a prelude to redundancies and unilaterally imposed changes in working systems and this view was undoubtedly justified by events. In truth, what happened was that job evaluations were made after a take-over or change in structure and there would have been redundancies in any event. Generally the same consultant performing the job evaluation also provided the system analysis. Given the nature of the exercise, it is clear that the results depend totally on the factors chosen and the weights that these factors are given. The union's job is to insist on being involved in the selection of these two items and then ensure that the job descriptions to which these factors are applied are accurate. This is a skilled and specialist task in the initial stages. White-collar unions have learned to become involved very early on. The case of women is one which shows the dangers of total reliance on the objectivity of job evaluation. It is not difficult to imagine a job evaluation which includes the factors of accuracy and unpleasant working conditions to find the latter considerably higher-rated than the former. As most of the women will be working in offices, they will get a low score as accuracy gets few points; the skills of typists or filing clerks rate few points. Women will thus be evaluated well down the scale.

It is easy to say that the union must manage this adequately. Realistically, union members themselves are not free from prejudice, and women need to be more than adequately represented on any panel of employees set up for job evaluation. However, consultancies themselves throw up an interesting, dangerous and yet under-publicised problem for white-collar unions. A consultancy will, most often, not only perform the job evaluation; it will also suggest salaries for each grade and contract to keep the employer up to date with external movements affecting these salaries. To this end the consultancy will do salary surveys amongst its own clients: an incestuous exercise. When a union sits down to negotiate, the company side then has a fixed position. In cases like these, it is with the consultancy that the union should be bargaining. This method of salary fixing is based exclusively on a market theory and a limited market to boot; it does not take into account profitability, productivity and overall higher levels of responsibility in one enterprise as compared with others. From a union point of view this is thus most unsatisfactory.

Unions, although the bulk of their work is in the industrial field, nevertheless do tend to use the mechanisms available in other parts of society and this applies particularly to white-collar unions. We have already pointed out the use of private parliamentary legislation, but there are many other avenues open. Many of the unions affiliated to the Labour Party sponsor Members of Parliament. This means providing funds to the constituency party, not to the Member, and it certainly does not mean control of the Member by the union. In addition to sponsorship most Labour MPs are members of unions, indeed the rule is that they must be. Many of them are members of the white-collar unions. At ASTMS there are thirty-six Labour MPs, and four Members of the House of Lords; all are members of the ASTMS parliamentary committee. In addition there are Tory and Liberal MPs and Members of the Lords who are also ASTMS members, but they have been uncooperative in the generality of the union's work. The parliamentary committee is a useful and vigorous part of the mechanism used by this union to defend its members' interests. Cases of closure or more usually potential closure, gross mismanagement, government legislation and suggestions for legislation are discussed. Matters affecting the union directly and indirectly are discussed, such as EEC affairs, the economy, worker participation and specific problems such as ICL computers, Chrysler and Norton-Villiers Triumph. The committee does not only discuss; once it agrees to do so, it acts. Early-day motions, deputations to Ministers, Private Members' bills, Ten-Minute-Rule bills, visits to plants and installations and amendments to bills to committee stage, all are new techniques available in the armoury.

Other white-collar unions have MPs as members, but do not utilise them on the same scale. But if one looks at the Cabinet as of December 1977, eleven were members of white-collar unions. TASS, APEX and ASTMS have Cabinet Ministers in membership. The union of today has to act as an American-style lobbyist at times and this can often be done alongside the parliamentary committee. Both delegations and written papers are presented to government departments and ministers on industry matters, on legislation and on specific complaints.

For example, over the past two years ASTMS alone has presented evidence on the telecommunications industry; the car industry in general, in evidence to the Select Committee; Chrysler and BMC; the problems of the NHS; difficulties over occupational pensions; the selection of nuclear power reactors; a new insurance company bill; the importation of television tubes; the Pilkington Glass Company; industrial deafness; Armed Forces unionisation; and a wide range of related issues. In many of the cases, the members produced the drafts and, rather than simply accept a resolution, the union used political means to achieve its ends. It cannot truthfully be said that each meeting or paper had the desired effect, but they certainly added to the debate and in many instances they affected the final report or outcome. Both the public and private sector unions are involved in public affairs; the TSSA objected and still objects strongly and publicly to the run-down of British Rail services and NALGO to the cuts in local government expenditure.

Historically, the Labour Party and the trade union movement have always been close. Many of the white-collar unions continue the tradition and are affiliated to the Labour Party. The affiliation is made through the deduction of a political levy on members from which members can freely contract out. It is a matter of regret that a relatively high percentage of members in the white-collar sector do contract out of this obligation, especially in view of the uses to which the money is put. The affiliation means that a union has the right to propose motions at the Labour Party Conference and theoretically through this mechanism form government policy, should there be a Labour Government. It also means that unions can also be represented on the Labour Party NEC policy formulating sub-committees.

Another extra-industrial tactic is the use of legal mechanisms. Few unions, white-collar or otherwise, either like to use the courts or are sanguine about their chances of success when they do. It is thus often a matter of the last resort. When the Industrial Relations Act was in operation, unions were dragged into the legal arena. Although the AUEW did not recognise the National Industrial Relations Court at all and, at the other end of the scale, NUBE used it aggressively, most TUC-affiliated unions attended to defend themselves if the occasion demanded. In the white-collar sector this meant defence against registered unions; as well as employers all of the ones concerned were quasi-unions who were attempting to use the Court to award bargaining rights in areas where TUC unions either had the rights or had a substantial membership. ASTMS defended itself in these, without the use of legal counsel, and fought off challenges at Rolls Royce and Associates, C. A. Parsons and British European Airways (as it then was). The Commission on Industrial Relations produced the reports for the Court and, by and large, it must be said that they were accurate and objective. In passing it is worth noting that in nearly all of these cases the employer joined with the TUC unions in opposing the claim for the simple reason that they had a stable industrial relations situation and did not wish it to be upset.

In one case, however, the positions were reversed. This was at ICI and is worth more than a cursory examination in that it had an enormous effect. ICI had been pursuing a steady policy of non-co-operation with white-collar unions for some years. They commissioned the highly controversial Tavistock Attitude Survey and the resulting confusion saw the emergence of two staff associations. The more junior of these overestimated itself and asked the company for sole bargaining rights for all white-collar staffs. Even ICI management refused this and the staff association then applied to the National Industrial Relations Court under Section 45 of the Industrial Relations Act. The major union involved was ASTMS, but TASS, APEX and ACTSS all had members involved.

The case was duly sent to the CIR for investigation. Soon after this the Government fell and the Industrial Relations Act was repealed and along with it the CIR was disbanded. However, the CIR report was produced before it wound up and it suggested that the TUC-affiliated union should have the bargaining rights in the large scientific area and left some others open pending union recruitment. ICI was then morally obliged when confronted with objective evidence to concede bargaining rights (after a long process) to a white-collar union for the first time. It is odd that this Act and this Section in particular, which was designed to hinder independent trade union growth, should through a series of accidents actually promote it in one of the most hostile of environments.

Unions have not always spurned legal action: injunctions have been applied for and granted and damages suits won for injuries and for industrial diseases. And in a series of notable instances ASTMS broke a government incomes policy with cases taken on behalf of members in County Courts alleging breach of contract where an employer refused to honour an agreement. This was in 1966 and has been well documented elsewhere.

A notable case of successful white-collar union pressure was (and indeed still is) the work done on fee-charging employment agencies. The International Labour Office has a convention demanding their disbandment since it considers that they have anti-social features. The ILO report states that the agencies place personnel in permanent or temporary jobs purely for the profit involved (sometimes this can be very high), with little or no thought for the career of the person concerned. Agencies have been used to strike-break, to hold back permanent staff salaries and have been deployed to fight trade union organisations. The non-manual workers in the TUC persuaded it to adopt a policy of abolition. Detailed evidence was given on the subject to a House of Commons Select Committee. Mr Kenneth Lewis introduced a Private Member's bill to exercise some degree of control and this was given government time and enacted. Since then the public-sector unions have taken up the challenge and not by lobbying: in the civil service they ran a series of strikes and blacked the work of agency staff; in the Health Service agency nurses must be paid the same as other nurses and not the premium that they were previously receiving. This campaign had some considerable success. It was not premised on the denial of the right of people to work intermittently if they choose to do so; it was premised on the immorality of making a profit out of that decision and the abuses which automatically stem from it.

The white-collar employee has seen his or her traditional differentials eroded. It is not only a white-collar problem. A NEDO study in February 1976 showed that earnings for unskilled and semi-skilled workers had overtaken those of the skilled in many instances. There is an argument, mainly propounded by those on the wilder fringe of the left, which applauds this as a move in the right direction with the ultimate being a situation where everyone is paid the same.

We live in a capitalist society in Britain. Profit is made and its ethic widely accepted. An employee who has a skill or responsibility will want to be paid for carrying it and the training-cum-experience which probably needed some considerable self-investment. Equal pay for all could, theoretically, mean that there would be no return on this investment and equally that would mean a diminution in the number of people acquiring skills or prepared to accept responsibility when something goes wrong. This would be discriminating against employees' rights whilst accepting the right of fixed capital to earn a return. We do not live in a society where people are prepared to work for the social good and nothing else and until we do (and this would require not only a political revolution but a revolution in attitudes), differentials are justified and this is all to the good. However, they have been shrinking and in some cases they have been reversed. The disposable, after-tax income situation is worse. Tax is an important consideration. The standard rate of tax is 33 per cent from £750 to £8,000 taxed income. At £8,000 it rises to 40 per cent, at £9,000 to 45 per cent, etc. The system adopted in Britain of allowing the progressive element to be made through non-taxed allowances means that the middle-income group earner is the most heavily burdened in relation to his or her ability to shoulder that burden. As a result of this, the non-taxable elements in remuneration have become more important for white-collar employees.

The salary package is now a well-established concept in the white-collar union world. Pensions, holidays, overtime, shift pay, concessionary mortgages, travel facilities, cars, discounts, vouchers, subsidies and better facilities, all are part of this package and we shall look at some of them in more detail in the next chapter. A good package can add as much as 60 per cent of the cost of the employee's salary to the employer's bill and this was recognised by the tax restrictions placed on them in the 1976 and 1977 Budgets.

An interesting development of the package, one tried in the US and now starting to be introduced in Britain, is the shopping basket approach. The employer offers a global sum of money to an employee who can then take it as salary and any selection of fringe benefits which, together, then add up to the global amount. The employee, however, is not immutably bound to the original choice; he or she can change at specified periods. For example, a young married man could maximise his concessionary mortgage facilities. When older he may switch this into stock options or prestige transport and when older still, to his pension provisions. To date, this system is only in operation for a handful of senior executives and is obviously quite difficult to administer as well as difficult to optimise. It does, however, give employees a larger degree of choice and any such scheme may be picked up by unions if it is in their members' interests.

The salary package has come at a time when the pressure is being put on employers by the manual workers' unions for 'single status' arrangements. These include demands for equal hours of work, equal holidays, bonuses and pension schemes and the non-pecuniary subjects such as not clocking on. The white-collar unions tend to welcome most of such moves, but not all, because some of them, like common pension arrangements, can work to the detriment of white-collar staffs unless care is taken. Providing that the overall differential is maintained, and this means that salary increases must be paid, then white-collar employees are quite satisfied. Incomes policies, where staff employees are deliberately being squeezed financially, are unfortunate situations to move to single status. If status is removed without adequate compensation, there may well be an uncontrollable explosion of white-collar militancy and noting the dispute details earlier, it is obviously not as far fetched as it sounds. It is also, given the changes in the structure of the labour force, probably likely to be more effective in disruptive terms than a comparable manual workers' campaign.

No one likes to be made redundant. The Protestant work ethic still grips Britain and the financial shortfall is difficult to bear. This book is being written at a time when unemployment is higher than any other time since the Second World War. Redundancy in the white-collar sector is a harsh phenomenon. Teachers and nurses, civil servants and local government personnel all thought themselves secure and with good historical precedents to assure them, but they were wrong. The growth in corporate back-up staff in departments such as 'research' and 'development and operations' has also meant that a company can economise on its salary bill whilst still having the same output by 'slimming' those departments.

Redundancies stem from three main, and basically different, sources. They may be part of a long- or short-term cost-cutting exercise often presented as an 'efficiency drive'; they may come as the result of a merger, or they may result from the winding up of a company or enterprise. Prevention is certainly better than cure in redundancy situations. The Employment Protection Act lays down minimum periods of notification in impending redundancies affecting more than ten employees and these periods rise to ninety days. There is now a statutory obligation laid upon managements to consult with their recognised unions and set out their reasons in writing. This gives unions the chance to influence events and, at the worst, provides time for employees to look for other jobs.

Ideally, a union will want to negotiate a 'no-involuntary' redundancy agreement. These are rare, but are on the increase. In one instance when the Prudential Assurance Company wished to reduce its staff it had to do so with a voluntary early retirement scheme. This is now a feature of all impending redundancies, but most employers offer singularly poor terms. The Prudential scheme had to be attractive to employees and thus not only has enhanced non-reduced pensions, but a lump sum benefit too, in all amounting to a considerable amount of money.

The white-collar unions generally have 'redundancy' or 'job security' agreements with employers. It is necessary to overcome fear on these occasions: very much like taking out an insurance policy – it is to cover against a situation which hopefully will not occur. These agreements generally include provisions stipulating a halt in recruitment and advertising for jobs, a commitment to placement within the organisation if possible, retraining and moving allowances and provisions for notice. Redundancy payments (well in excess of the statutory arrangements), pensions, counselling services, early retirements and the method of selection, are also normal. If this does not eliminate the need for redundancy it certainly removes part of the pain, as employees pass out through a money-shaped aperture. The Woolwich agreement with GEC, after its take-over of AEI, was the forerunner of these agreements at the end of the 1960s, but improvements have been made in all respects since then.

A company closure is quite another matter. For reasons of commercial viability these are often not announced until the decision has been taken. If a redundancy agreement exists, well and good; if not, there can be problems. The Upper Clyde shipbuilders work-in started a new form of industrial action, one that has been repeated again and again. The idea is to preserve the production capability intact, until a new buyer comes along, whilst still producing and selling the goods. On occasions workers' co-operatives have been set up. The unions involved will certainly lobby and meet the Department of Industry, try to get grants, ask for National Enterprise Board funding, attempt to get subsidised or short-time working try to get competitive imports stopped.

It might now be alleged fairly that alert unions with new ideas are basically the only organisations fighting for the future of British industry as opposed to short-term profits. They do so in defence of the membership of the enterprise in question, but in so doing also defend the living standards of all the British people in the future.

Chapter 6

The rewards system

'A chicken in every pot and two cars in every garage' – Calvin Coolidge

Like society in general, industrial relations are continually changing and evolving. Technological advances bring ranges of new products and services to the marketplace; they also change work patterns and demand new negotiating techniques. In so many respects white-collar trade unionism is a new concept. Certainly, it has existed for over one hundred years, but its acceptance in such great measure is new and still not total. The shift in demand is towards the professional approach rather than the older understandable, visceral reaction. The growing change in emphasis from the traditional short-term reaction position to the long-term pre-emption of options is a reflection of society's changing attitudes. The old-style trade unionist sitting baffled by jargon on a government enquiry or on the board of an agency has given way to vigorous representation by well-equipped and well-backed advocates.

The media, notably television, have played their part in the gradual illumination of political figures, as they have to cope with probing interviews in the fullest of public gazes. The trade unionist is subjected to this ordeal but with the difference that he or she does not have the same reputation to lose; articulation, sensibility and intelligence are projected where prejudice had denied their existence. The white-collar employees used to be the largest reservoir of public opinion in the population which reinforced hostility to the unions, but slowly and surely that is being transformed to active support.

Whilst the media give a new, and essentially positive, exposure to the bargainers, they also bring exposure of salary settlements, new ideas and new agreements. Non-unionised people have begun to realise how much they are missing because they now have the data that used to be obscured by a reluctance to disclose personal salary levels. Union members realise, too, what their colleagues are getting and put in claims for the same thing – with expedition. British society is acquisitive and based on rising expectations and it is not alone. All societies have this approach, but these expectations can only be fulfilled out of income and so the basic work of the trade union is nothing more than a response to society's needs, although there is a leadership function on other matters.

Their horizons are widening and the salary package and a more sophisticated type of negotiation is now becoming the bread-and-butter issue of white-collar union work. In Chapter 5 we mentioned the package and some of the elements in it, now it is necessary to open it up in more detail.

The salary package may be a slight misnomer. It suggests that all the elements in it are negotiated simultaneously but this is quite often not the case. The package is often negotiated, item by item, in separate negotiations and entered into separate agreements over a long time scale. There are exceptions to this, of course. The basic salary, overtime premiums and holidays are often settled in the basic negotiating round. There are advantages and disadvantages in a total-package settlement. The major advantage is that trade-offs of one demand and one response for another can be made more visibly and easily and both management and employees know exactly where they stand. The main disadvantage is that it may well be easier to negotiate one benefit at a time and thus to get marginally better settlements purely because of the undivided attention that one element gets. From an industrial action point of view, should it be needed, the single element of negotiation is by far the most preferable as it presents clear issues – the package can be blurred and difficult to explain. Whichever method is chosen, the package now exists and we must look at some of the more common elements.

Holiday entitlements have been negotiated steadily since the growth of organised trade unions, often slowly and frequently painfully. This book cannot really deal with quantitative aspects of either schemes or other benefits – by the time it is actually published they should be out of date and superseded by better norms. Overtime and shift payments are, however, another matter. The majority of white-collar staff either have no chance to earn these payments or have little opportunity outside the operations of transport enterprises, foremen tied to shop-floor shifts and hours, or computer complexes. If the moves to equal status continue, the movement will certainly be for staff and managers to get overtime and shift payments on the same basis as the manual workers. The present situation often depends on the willingness and goodwill of staff and managers but this attitude is changing; the managers at the Midland Bank, for example, have put in a claim for overtime payments.

The most expensive single item in the package is often the pension scheme. A good one can cost anything up to 20 per cent plus of a payroll. White-collar unions have been actively negotiating occupational pension schemes for up to twenty years, although as legislation changes – and it has frequently – so union tactics and objectives have had to be modified. Manual workers' unions have traditionally been far less interested in pensions (other than the recent T&GWU campaign on state pensions), and although this is changing marginally as the G&MWU, for example, employs expert pensions officers, it is still basically true. This is exemplified both by the uninterest that manual workers tend to have in occupational schemes along with their unwillingness to pay more as a contribution and by the traditional view that unions should contract into the new state second-tier pension scheme. Certainly most, if not all, white-collar unions will disregard this advice and contract out whilst continuing to run the occupational scheme alongside the state scheme.

'Single status' is often built around a common pension scheme and as we explained earlier the white-collar union attitude can be summed up by 'fine, but not at our expense'. In pension schemes you simply get what you pay for. By and large, manual workers have not been ready to contribute more than 3 per cent of salary while staff expect to contribute up to 6 per cent and this, in itself, is a stumbling block. It is, however, possible to overcome it by using a two-tier scheme and not by trying, as some companies have, to split the difference and have a scheme which suits neither party. The contracting-in problem is, however, quite different. This cannot be solved by companies; either the scheme is contracted-in or it is not. Manual workers will be advised to contract-in by their unions, white-collar staff will be urged to contract-out. In this event the only solution is to run two separate schemes, open to both sides, which will divide, not entirely but nearly, on a staff-manual worker basis.

Briefly, what a white-collar union will demand is to get as near to the Inland Revenue limits as possible and any shortfall will represent a target for future negotiations. Final salary accruing at one-sixtieth (or one-fiftieth in the better cases) per year of service, two-thirds widows', widowers', and dependants' and orphans' benefits, life assurances, long-term disability pension, commutation and employee trustees. This last point is one of principle rather than of money. The monies held in trust are held for members of the scheme, yet up to five years ago one could count the number of private companies with employee trustees on the fingers of one hand. This has changed and is changing at some speed, as a few of them already have 50 per cent employee trustees with an independent chairman. Logically, this is only proper. As the money is held in trust for members only, why should the member be precluded from having some control over its disposition? Equally, if pensions are deferred income, and more and more this is becoming the accepted view, why should this income be considered to be totally out of the control of its owner?

There are many other elements of the package. Some employers, especially in the finance sector, provide concessionary mortgage arrangements with interest rates ranging from 2·5 to 4 per cent. At a time when commercial rates are running between 9 and 10 per cent this is a very great benefit and can indeed be looked upon as increased disposable income. Company cars are another element. These can be provided in total with petrol or mileage allowances — loaned, partly paid for, or the benefit can be just running cost allowances for a privately owned car. The motor car manufacturing companies have a discount purchasing scheme for most categories of their own workers.

Vouchers are another element. Luncheon vouchers are a standard benefit in London but there are also holiday vouchers, cleaning vouchers, theatre vouchers, indeed a whole range which are available from employers. British Rail provide free travel for employees and their families and British Airways provide very low-cost flights. The 1976 Budget may have caught many of these benefits (only time and Inland Revenue decisions will tell) but there is bound to be a justifiable resistance as these have long been an element in the remuneration package. There are share-option schemes, too, but these must be approached with a degree of caution. Many of these schemes involve a financial risk to the employee and the basic union feeling is that being dependent on an employer for income is bad enough without compounding it by being dependent on the savings side too. The April 1978 Budget Concessions on tax payable for worker/shareholders is so marginal as to make no difference to this attitude. Allowances, such as responsibility allowances for taking over a more senior employee's responsibilities for some time, are also part of the package. There are more highly specialised allowances in Britain: a carbon-black dirty allowance at Dunlop, a Mersey ferry and bosun's-chair allowance at Shell, and a snow allowance at the Fylingdales early-warning radar station. More conventionally, maternity leave is now almost standard and the Employment Protection Act will ensure that it is; paternity leave is now in some agreements and crêches at the place of work are becoming a reality where practicable, or payments towards crêche facilities where not.

The number of hours of work are certainly part of the package and these have been falling consistently. The London office worker works 34–36½ hours per week. However, a manager may voluntarily put in as much as 60 hours, a doctor 80 hours, whilst a foreman works the same hours as those being supervised. In the past few years, however, many flexitime schemes have been introduced. Flexitime is designed around the principle of certain fixed hours and some variable hours either side of this. Hours can be carried forward, generally on a monthly basis. Flexitime has disadvantages but it does have the great asset of suiting many women whose time is constrained by school hours. It is difficult to adapt flexitime to productive processes, especially those using a continuous-line process, and as a result this system has not affected many manual workers' unions.

Non-pecuniary elements play their part in the package. Internal status is often measured by carpet size, curtains, type of filing cabinet, and among other things, there is the label of the tailor who can be used, or the restaurant or canteen that can be eaten in, and so on. White-collar unions neither condone these fringe benefits nor negotiate them. They are used to establish status without remuneration and as they generally apply to the middle or upper echelons of staff, this prevents the lower echelon establishing their proper monetary differentials. The in-work environment is, however, the proper preserve of the union. Not only must the Shops, Offices and Railway Premises Act provisions be observed, but the temperature must conform to standards, too. More recently unions have been involved in new office designs, and in some instances the location of offices or computer installations.

A white-collar union generally has to cope with performance appraisal techniques in a formalised setting. These are far more prevalent in staff areas where there are no genuine bench-marks against which to measure an employee's contributional performance. Performance appraisal has, however, been the subject of considerable abuse in the past. Critical assessments have been written on employees to settle personal grudges or to facilitate the removal of union activists. Up to the time that trade unions started to organise, appraisals were secret documents, and preferment or otherwise was made by leaning heavily on reports which the employee concerned had never seen and was thus not capable of challenging. Since then the systems have, in great measure, become more open. The usual procedure is that the appraisals are made at a set time on standardised forms. When completed the document is shown to the employee who is given the opportunity to check it and, if necessary, argue with it. If the employee is satisfied the form is initialled and passed up the line. If not, there is an appeal procedure to a higher ranked manager.

This open system was fought for and disputes arose over it, because it can have two important bearings on the employee's working life. The first is that promotion boards often lean heavily on the evidence in the appraisals and, second, remuneration may depend upon it. In the white-collar field the ethos of a 'rate for the job' generally applies only to some basic clerical work. For the most part the salaries progress through a range on a yearly incremental basis; in many instances, such as local government and the Civil Service, this is an automatic procedure. In other instances in the private sector the movement is partly or wholly based on 'merit'.

The system can vary. In the Midland Bank there are three distinct incremental increases depending on performance appraisal but with published scales for all of them. In other cases there are merit-bands, a published top and bottom of the scale, but the actual merit increase paid is never published. In other cases all merit incremental increases are totally secret. Yet another variant is to have an incremental scale, but to have secret merit increases paid on top of this. Some consultancies recommend merit measurement as the standard method; others refuse to trade in it. Most of the unions involved dislike merit payments, they believe that if an employee is doing the job, he or she should be paid for it and if some are doing it better and more enthusiastically than others, then they should be promoted. In local government the habit is for such employees to miss out a step in the scale and get a double increment. The whole concept of increments is based on the theory that experience is necessary for the adequate performance of duties; a person is judged to be not as completely effective in the job after one year as he or she will be after four years and therefore it would be invidious to pay both a one- and a five-year employee the same salary. Most members and most unions accept this with reservations. Merit payments, however, are still approved by some white-collar staff and despite the unions' objection to them in principle, ranges of award are negotiated. By definition, only a few can get high merit payments as the comparison is made on an internal- and not an external-objective basis and even if the overall standard is high, only those with the highest standard will get top merit payment. It really boils down to a method of management for getting the most amount of work for the minimum of cost.

Bonuses of all descriptions are often merit-type payments. In one of the most under-unionised sectors of the economy embracing the Stock Exchange and brokers' offices, the system is to pay low salaries to the majority of staff but have an annual bonus related to profits over the year; this can be more than 100 per cent of salary. Consultants in hospitals have a merit-award system and although this is on a published scale, the awards are made secretly and again, the merit award may double the basic salary. Finally, merit payments cause friction between the staff – this is described as either motivation or competitive spirit, but industrial relations must suffer from the suffocating effects of secrecy.

Productivity bargaining was stimulated in the white-collar sector by the Labour Government policies of 1967–70. Whilst basic salaries were restrained, increases based on productivity were allowable and so, to avoid being left even further behind, white-collar unions started to bargain on a productive basis but how is productivity measured in a staff environment? Most productive processes can have measurable increases in physical output and after adjustments have been made for inter-departmental flows and perhaps new machinery, an easily identifiable increase can be isolated. Output based on productivity deals on a fee per item basis can be easily handled. None of these can, however, be applied satisfactorily to most of the white-collar sector. Typists are an exception in that there is a measurable output generally expressed in 'lines' and productivity bargaining is well established in this field. But what of an insurance clerk, a bank teller or a research and development scientist? How can a union establish their measurable productivity increases? It is worse in the public sector. What constitutes productivity for a Department of Employment conciliator, a social worker or a doctor in a hospital?

The problems involved have led to a great deal of ingenious innovation from both sides of the bargaining table. Some of the schemes are nothing less than profit-sharing schemes expressed in new language. Others are based on rational standards of departmental duties. It was realised at quite an early point that most of the companies did not have an internal accounting system capable of generating enough suitable data on which to base adequate deals. Even companies with the sophisticated internal mechanisms of major financial institutions had difficulties in this respect. The result, at the Prudential and in other financial houses, is that the schemes are an approximation and based on work done over and above a fixed parameter adjusted for the number of employees. As employers cannot affect the inflow of work, (in insurance this is dependent on macro-economic factors) the scheme revolves around the number of staff employed in any one department. It is interesting to note that Phases II and III of the Counter-Inflation Policy in 1973 had a very complicated and detailed section on productivity bargaining. Most experts in the field felt it was impossible for any company in Britain to have fulfilled all the conditions laid down as their resources would not have allowed them to do so.

In 1977/8 the government once again began to examine increases in productivity on a 'self-financing basis'. From the union point of view, 60 per cent of employees are in the non-productive sectors and nearly 50 per cent in the white-collar employments and it looks as though the problem of payment is about to be revived again. Considerable damage has already been done by income policy restrictions, which have been interpreted so extremely as to limit commission for salesmen who have physically sold more goods and services at home and abroad. We shall look at this in greater detail in Chapter 8.

Arbitration is a familiar form of settling disputes in the white-collar sector. It is the standard method for settling differences in the civil service, has been used extensively in local government, railways and in some parts of the private sector, such as banking. With the advent of the ACAS and the CAC (the formal arbitration arm of ACAS) it is very probable that this approach will be used more. But, it may not be noticed because of its lack of a gladiatorial quality, its relative non-newsworthiness and, thus, its anonymity.

On the theory that an arbiter will always compromise, it pays the union to demand more than it thinks it will get, the employer to offer less than he thinks will be accepted and wait for the arbiter to split the difference. In practical terms this has led to these particular industries and organisations lagging behind in pay levels for, roughly, four out of every five years and to have a catch-up year in the fifth. Obviously, this puts such staff at a disadvantage in cash-flow terms. Few militantly led, non-manual union agreements have this final clause, although it must be realised that its absence does not *preclude* arbitration. But this generally comes, as with the manual unions, after an intractable dispute; not instead of a dispute. We noted the problems in preparing an arbitration case in Chapter 4 and all there is left to add is that great care must be taken in selecting the arbiter or the arbitration panel.

One tactic, seemingly used only by the newer unions but of great value, is to attend the annual general meeting of a company in which the union has members. ASTMS keeps a portfolio of shares in all its major negotiating adversaries, not for investment purposes but for the handful of shares required to gain an entry to the meeting. It is clearly an embarrassment for a board of directors, especially if they are in other difficulties, to have an articulate trade union official explain to the shareholders present at the meeting the shortcomings of their industrial relations policy and how this is affecting the running of the company. When the US Chrysler Corporation bought up the residual British-owned shares in 1972 an extraordinary general meeting had to be held. One of the authors attended this meeting (the only trade unionist to do so) and explained the union's objections to the proposals (in hindsight these were only too justified). Although the deal went through because of the approval of the Conservative Government, the ASTMS intervention forced a hearing in the High Court and it is now on record that some people foresaw the Chrysler crisis of 1976 and its eventual take-over in 1978.

Horizons are widening in membership terms, too. Each successive year brings groups in the trade union movement which previously had been considered unorganisable. Part of this is is due to government policies and potential policies. Employee directors and participation will undoubtedly stimulate trade union membership. Both the Industrial Relations Act and the Employment Protection Act contain statements urging employers to recommend trade union membership. In a whole range of activities, from pensions to redundancy, managements are now charged with consulting the appropriate independent trade unions before any action can be taken. If an employee wishes to have any control over his or her working life, then membership of an independent trade union is becoming the only possible vehicle. This obviously applies in greater measure to those enterprises with no such recognised salaried staff unions like IBM and Michelin. However, it also applies across whole groupings of employees, whether middle-management, engineers, architects or other professional occupations within companies who either have to rely on unions doing the work for them (with policies over which they have no control) or join a union and exercise their democratic rights to influence decisions.

Whilst recruitment within the 'professions' has been slow, changes are now taking place. In the ante-chamber of the professions, unions have signed agreements with the NUS concerning student membership; this is an important step forward. ASTMS has negotiated locally for some time on behalf of graduate students who had posts as research assistants or associates. This agreement allows the union to recruit both graduates and undergraduate students on the understanding that it will not conflict in any way with normal NUS representation. This is a radically new departure. Most students (other than those in the specific disciplines like medicine, law and engineering) have little, if any idea, of what jobs they may occupy when they leave university. It is a reasonable estimate that in the future these potential managers and professional workers will not only have a better idea of what trade unionism is all about but will retain membership throughout their working lives.

The horizons are widening in all directions. Across nations and through the traditional status boundaries of British life. Simultaneously the horizons in bargaining itself are about to be radically extended and the white-collar unions will have a singular and important role to play.

Chapter 7

New legislation

'Laws are like cobwebs, which may catch small flies, but let wasps and hornets break through.' – Swift

1975 was a year of economic and political contrasts. The first Referendum held in the UK divided political parties and strained relationships, unemployment rose steadily to over one million, output fell, real disposable incomes fell, the TUC underwrote the £6 pay limit and the list of bankruptcies lengthened. Yet 1975 also saw more new legislation, directives and orders in council with an influence on industrial relations, collective bargaining and trade union activities of all kinds than in any similar period. Their impact will fall in great measure on white-collar unions, although obviously the effect will be felt by all trade unions.

All British people live and work within a framework of laws, some enacted by parliament and some which have evolved through the common law system. No matter what the job, where one lives or how old one is, this framework acts as a constraint on the activities of the people, channelling them in directions in which they themselves might not want to go but in which society believes they should go. Perhaps this should be better phrased as the direction society *believed* they should go, as political and social *mores* often change well in advance of the appropriate legislative changes.

The recent past has seen a quite incredible switch in trade union attitudes which has been reflected in legislation. The pace of change has been quite remarkable, paralleling the changes in technology and its social impact over the same brief period. British unions traditionally took the view that the voluntary collective bargain was superior to a statute. Clearly, this could no longer be said to hold good in the field of health and safety. The key stimulus to accepting and indeed promoting change was the union reaction to the Heath Government's 1971 Industrial Relations Act. But in so many other areas it was in any event clear that the UK had become visibly deficient in the field of social reform.

Trade unions are not exempt from total legal changes and have been prime targets. The 1971 Industrial Relations Act attempted to codify,

95

control, delineate and then effectively to emasculate trade unions. It was out of joint with the times but was an inadvertent catalyst – the unions started to look for measures which affirmed their rights and met their new needs. The 1971 Act was repealed by the Trade Unions and Labour Relations Act, 1974, which, however, re-enacted and amended their unfair dismissal procedures, a most important section especially for white-collar unions. Basically, the law reverted to the situation just prior to the 1971 Act. Then in 1975 the Employment Protection Act was enacted and will be discussed at greater length below. At roughly the same time the Sex Discrimination Act and the Industry Act both obtained Royal Assent with the Health and Safety Act and Social Security Pensions Act only recently on the statute book. In the Autumn of 1976, the government announced its intention to legislate in the field of industrial democracy and appointed a committee of inquiry, taking as its starting point the TUC's proposal for worker directors to have half the seats on company boards. The resulting *Bullock Majority Report* was the centre of the debate and possible legislation. The focal point is now the Government White Paper *Industrial Democracy* (Command 7231), which represents a retreat from the Bullock proposals and builds in a large delay before legislation can be enacted. Nevertheless, the commitment to change remains. Together these developments widen bargaining areas, redefine the scope of union responsibilities, employees' rights and employers' duties, and add some measure of protection to both employees and their representative organisations. In short, there will now be a very different set of relationships with which both unions and employers will have to become familiar. Much of the new legislation particularly affects non-manual trade unions as it creates new privileges and duties precisely in their fields.

The Employment Protection Act was finally enacted on 12 November 1975, after a series of very late night sittings, controversial amendments, House of Lords obstructionism and bitter debate. As an Act it is a collection of new ideas and approaches, stemming from three distinct causes. One was that the Act was based upon a series of TUC propositions drawn up as part of the Social Contract with the Labour Government and planners before the election of that government in 1974. The second is that the Act recognises that good industrial relations stem from the removal of the trigger points causing friction between the parties. As these encompass a great variety of grievances, the Act ranges over what on the surface appears to be a remarkably disparate set of topics. This approach is philosophically more apt for ameliorating industrial relations problems than that used by the Industrial Relations Act which concentrated solely on the mechanics of trade unions and draconian controls. Good industrial relations cannot exist isolated from an overall approach to enfranchise the worker in the workplace. This is the third concept and, in Scandinavia, legislation has moved on from excellent labour *protection* statutes towards more representation, leading clearly to managerial co-determination. The UK Employment Protection Act only just starts moving in that direction and it is interesting, as an index of the undeveloped nature of British thinking in this area, to note that this legislation benefits the unions far less than the 1971 Industrial Relations Act benefited employees. The Employment Protection Act, which is very long (207 pages, 129 sections and 18 schedules), can be divided into the provisions which will affect all unions and those that will mainly affect the non-manual sector. The guaranteed payments provisions almost exclusively affect manual employees as nearly all (if not all) white-collar workers do not lose money in the event of stoppages and the itemised pay statement is a normal procedure in white-collar employment. The wages councils and statutory joint industrial councils proposals are, and will be, provisions almost exclusively affecting low-paid manual workers in some industries with poor union organisation and an inferior bargaining position. The majority of the sections, however, will affect the entire trade union movement although some will be of special and almost exclusive interest to the white-collar sector. The first major change is the statutory basis given to the ACAS and the formation of the CAC. The ACAS was set up in September 1974, to replace the Commission on Industrial Relations but this Act defines its duties and gives it precise powers. The Act also creates a separate Certification Officer whose duty it is to issue Certificates of Independence to trade unions who wish to apply for them. We dealt with the deficiencies in this part of the legislation in Chapter 3.

When an employer refuses to recognise a union, an application for recognition can be made to ACAS under Section 11 of the Employment Protection Act, first to settle the matter by conciliation. If the employer concedes, the matter rests there but more often these attempts fail. The ACAS may then use any measure it thinks fit to determine the validity of the claim; these will include ballots, attitude surveys and interviews. At the end of the investigation there is either a recommendation for recognition or a written report specifying why the applicant should not be recognised. If, after a recommendation has been made, the employer refuses to comply, a reference may be made to the CAC and part of this complaint may include a claim for specific terms and conditions of service on behalf of the members. If the employer still refuses recognition the CAC will arbitrate on the claim and make a legally binding award to the union. This sting in the tail should help undermine the employer's resistance as it provides an end point to the procedures. But, clearly, if a rogue management maintained its opposition to formal recognition and had to be referred regularly to the CAC, the law would have to be revised. At the moment, it rests on the hope that employers will recognise the balance of advantage.

The Grunwick dispute demonstrated this point quite clearly. The managing director did not allow ACAS to interview his employees in the plant and ACAS has no power to compel any employer to do so; or indeed to divulge the names and addresses of employees or make any relevant computer personnel roles available. The problems at Grunwick stemmed partly from this action. It is clear that legislation of this sort is based on the notion of reasonable parties, once one side takes an albeit legally defensible nihilist position the legislation breaks down.

However, the Grunwick affair only demonstrated in a dramatic way what most white-collar unions had already noticed. Employer procrastination has been practised widely and ACAS has no powers to deal with it. Some cases have been at ACAS for eighteen months and are still not resolved. This is partly due to understaffing and partly due to the quality of staffing although it must, in fairness, be said that many of the old CIR hands who transferred over are both perceptive and diligent. It is however basically due to employers delaying ballots, losing computer discs, or changing the concept of the bargaining unit. Obviously, this is in the interests of the employer. As we explained earlier, trade union membership tends to melt away when recognition is not forthcoming and this is precisely what is in the so uncooperative employers' minds.

Not all decisions under the procedure have been universally acclaimed. At the General Accident Insurance Company, ACAS awarded separate bargaining rights, one to APEX and the other to ASTMS. This was despite a history of recognition attempts by ASTMS against the most hostile of employers whilst APEX had no such history. It was despite a report which showed an overwhelming majority of employees wanted to be represented by ASTMS (even many APEX members) and despite a report favouring ASTMS.

One final point on recognition – a legal point. It is one thing to have legislation attempting to give collective rights, it is another to make it stick in the courts. Judges traditionally view themselves as protecting individual rights and view a collective right as removing individual rights unless there is 100 per cent approval – a most unlikely circumstance. Cases such as Grunwick and the ACAS and Legal and General Insurance Company bear this out. As white-collar unions typically make more use of the legal provisions available this attitude, a nineteenth-century liberal one, has more effect on them than on other unions.

The second major point concerning white-collar unions is the unfair dismissal procedures. These were initiated under the ill-starred Industrial Relations Act, 1971, maintained in the Trade Unions and Labour Relations Act, 1974 and have been refined in this latest Act. The white-collar employees are not yet as militant as their manual colleagues (although they are catching up fast) and the possibilities of industrial action to press for reinstatement of a dismissed person are correspondingly reduced. This is even more the case where a union activist has been sacked for reasons which were partially connected with these activities but in a situation where the union is not strong enough to get recognition. There are still regularly recurring disputes over such issues throughout the manufacturing industry. It is now unfair to dismiss an employee for the reasons of independent union membership, for taking part in an industrial dispute, or for union activities within the scope of a procedure agreement. It is also unfair to dismiss an employee who refuses to join a non-independent trade union.

The final legal decision on the Grunwick case virtually makes the Section 11 recognition provisions inoperable. Few, if any, new references are being made to ACAS as it is clear that non-cooperation by an employer is a legally valid system despite the fact that ACAS is charged in Section 1(2) of the Act with 'promoting the improvement of industrial relations, and in particular of encouraging the extension of collective bargaining'. Many suggestions have been made to remedy this unfortunate state of affairs. One such is to increase the powers of ACAS to compel co-operation but this has been rejected; another is to abolish the section altogether and yet another to widen the power of ACAS to include words such as 'to the best of its ability'. At the time of writing this matter is still far from resolved.

These protections are valuable, although commonplace, in other countries. The industrial tribunals can now be urged to make reinstatement and re-engagement their main weapons. Damages can be awarded and, in cases of unfair dismissal for trade union reasons, these are higher. If an employer refuses to reinstate or re-engage the employee, then further positive damages may be awarded. The white-collar unions are hoping that these procedures, along with the references to the ACAS for recognition, and the realisation that so many listed organisations are anything but independent trade unions, will promote both recruitment and higher standards of living for the employees concerned. Alongside this run the new provisions on trade union membership and activities, which attempt to stop employers taking action short of dismissal against employees to inhibit them from trying to join an independent union, to stop them from taking part in union activities or to force them to join a non-independent body. An employee in this unfortunate position can apply to an industrial tribunal and, if the case is proved, can get compensation based on expenses and loss of benefits due to the employer's action.

As we explained earlier, as the white-collar unions expand in size so there becomes a greater need to educate their members. The provisions in this Act allowing independent trade unions' members reasonable time off for both industrial relations and educational activities are thus very timely. The education courses must be approved by either the TUC or the members' union, which should also stop employers from insisting on their own in-house variations on an industrial relations theme. These provisions apply to union officials and the time off is with pay. The ACAS was charged with producing a code on this subject.

This became operative on 1 April 1978, and is a totally unexceptional document. The code of practice is a strange instrument: it is not law, neither is it legally binding: it can, however, be used in evidence in legal proceedings. The codes (as applying to industrial relations) started with the generalised one attached to the Industrial Relations Act. This was a sort of Salvation Army exercise, a moral, right-thinking and eminently sober document which, unlike the Salvation Army, did no one any good and saved not one soul.

This latest code is unhappy in that it qualifies a right. Union officials have a right to paid time off and the code modifies this. The composition of ACAS makes such a qualification inevitable as does its 'soundings' procedure. Fortunately, the constraints are slight, as indeed is the assistance that it provides. In short, it will probably have the same impact as it predecessor – very little.

Providing it is realised that both the Act and the code lay down minimum standards, there is no problem. Many white-collar unions have agreements with employers for time off with pay for attending union educational courses. The Act only extends this right to union officials and ASTMS for one has already had a local difficulty with this clause. The definition of 'official' is imprecise and basically one needs to educate members *before* they become officials. Thus whole new sections of quasi-union officials are being spawned by this section of the Act.

One sub-section of the code has drawn attention to a problem that may have been better left alone. Time off for union activities attracts no pay whilst that for collective-bargaining duties does. It is often difficult and always contentious to separate the two yet the code recommends that this is done. All good employers, and most of the indifferent ones, have evolved a system of closing a blind eye to this problem, the loss to the employer in productive terms is minuscule, the gain in goodwill immense. To harden this line would be provocative.

Trade union members will now have the right to reasonable time off, without pay, to conduct their union business. This may be of great assistance in finding suitable people for branch officials posts, where, in the past, there may have been an inadequate number of volunteers – it should also bring more women into trade union activities. A new impetus will also be given to claims for the secondment of branch officers in large establishments to full-time union work, paid for by the employers. The next few years will see the classic full-time shop stewards' convener flanked by his non-manual equivalent with his own office and secretarial assistance. The cost of educating them will be formidable and difficult to meet by the traditionally underfinanced British unions, who are now starting to alter their traditional educational patterns and to consider what level of state aid in this field should be available. It exists in other industrialised economies, most notably in Sweden where the present high level of assistance from the government was supplemented in 1977 by a payroll tax of 0·05 per cent, which should yield £10 million annually. Even the French Government pays more per year to one union centre, CGT, than the whole TUC receives.

The new provisions for the notifications of redundancies have been noted. They affect all unions and all categories of employees. If an employer fails to give the necessary period of notice and fails to consult about and give the reasons for the redundancies, a protective award may be made by the industrial tribunal. As with most other sections in the Act, a union in this instance means an 'independent trade union'. This award means that the employer has to continue to pay remuneration to the employee for the period specified in the award. If an employer fails to notify the DoE of impending redundancies, there may be a reduction in the redundancy payments rebate due to the employer although this cannot be more than 10 per cent of the rebate. This arose in April 1978 in the redundancies announced by Spillers French Baking Limited: no notice was given, a protective award was 'arranged' with the knowledge of the DoE and a reduction in the rebate was actively contemplated.

The new provisions on company failures, which are the cause of so many redundancies, also apply to the totality of unions and employees in the private sector. There have always been great difficulties in liquidation situations in ensuring that employees receive all the monies that are due to them for the work that they had done or expenses they had incurred. The employee used only to be a preferred creditor for up to £200, if the money was there, and thereafter joined the queue of unpreferred creditors. But in some notorious situations of 'administrative inadvertence', pension-fund contributions had been deducted from salaries and never paid over. The Redundancy Payments Fund will now pay wages and up to eight weeks' pay in lieu of notice, holiday pay, unfair dismissal compensation (if applicable) and unpaid contributions to pension schemes.

The new provisions on information are also helpful if, as explained earlier, arduous and challenging to research departments. The white-collar unions are often forced into the position of having to prepare very detailed claims to employers. The right of a trade union to information without which a union would be impeded in its collective bargaining and which should be supplied 'in accordance with good industrial relation practice' is thus an important one to white-collar unions. There are exemptions in the cases of national security, information on an individual without consent or on commercial grounds. The ACAS have provided a code of practice on this subject, too, and this came into operation in August 1977.

This code has a far more constraining effect than does the 'time off' one. A right has been conferred by the Act, but the code suggests it is inoperable in several cases The main problem arises with the notion of 'commercial damage'. An employer can claim almost anything causes commercial damage where a union is concerned, let alone releasing information. In earlier drafts the code suggests 'information agreements', but this has now been dropped under pressure from the CBI, presumably because they do not wish to formalise a situation they dislike.

Information is needed to present to members, not to present to the company in a claim. It would be foolish, would it not, to ask a management for information and then present it back to them the following day? Most managements protest that they already provide their employees with information and this many of them certainly do. This takes the form of 'pop accounts' simplified to the extent that they are meaningless; it arrives in the form of a section head pep talk and it arrives in the form of unnecessarily complicated and deliberately obscurantist presentations.

Unions want to have the raw material and present the facts as they see them. This does not preclude employers presenting them in their fashion; they undoubtedly will continue to do so but it does give the union member a wider interpretation and, thus, knowledge of what is happening in the workplace. A simple example of this can be seen in the T&GWU claim to the Ford Motor Company, challenging the current cost-accounting method used by the company; and they employed leading stockbrokers to do it for them. The T&GWU claimed an under-estimate of profits. In more general terms, the problem is that the profit has been redefined as capital and put into the balance sheet. This sort of tactic is the justification for unions wishing to present the facts themselves.

Although the information required will depend largely on the procedure agreement, unions will want unconsolidated management accounts; group (multinational or otherwise) transfer pricing; global profit data; tax liabilities excluding advanced corporation tax; man-power plans; investment plans; banded details of pay systems; merit and bonus payments; corporate plans and a host of smaller details in specific circumstances. Fortunately, the code of practice is of the same opinion, though where the concept of 'commercial damage' intervenes, can only be seen in the long run. If an employer fails to comply with the Act and a case presented to the CAC is successful, exactly the same remedy exists as with failure to recognise a union; that is, a legally binding award of terms and conditions of service may be made. Several white-collar unions have made claims under this section and have been refused the information required. At present several cases are with the CAC for adjudication, notably from NUBE, APEX, and ASTMS.

It is difficult to determine how well these provisions are working in practice as few claims have been to the CAC for arbitration. Early claims have shown up some glaring defects in the provisions: for example, companies need not provide information about salaries which they have obtained from a consultancy, even though these are used in job evaluations. A full claim against Beechams Pharmaceutical Divison is, at the present, with the CAC having been totally rejected by the management and is, in effect, a 'test case'.

The maternity leave provisions in the Act are part and parcel of equal opportunities for women as it is obvious that without this leave there cannot possibly be equal opportunity. We shall, therefore, look at this alongside another new piece of legislation: the Sex Discrimination Act.

The white-collar sector is characterised by its promotion ladders and a general preoccupation with them. Women employees simply do not get promoted in anything like the numbers that their involvement would indicate. Obviously, some women choose not to try for a career, as indeed do some men. It would be strange if more women than men were not in this category because the demands made by marriage, childbearing and childrearing conflict with work requirements. This is not a male chauvinist argument. The education system, the indoctrination by parents, the demands of husbands, or men in general, all reinforced by advertising techniques, have ensured that this conflict exists. Equal opportunities is not about *making* women have a career; this is no more liberating than making them stay at home with the children. It is about giving a full and proper choice. Without maternity leave this choice is an empty one.

Childbearing can, obviously, create a hiatus in a woman's career. In the past, not only has her job not been kept open for her after the birth but employers have anticipated a non-serious return to work and thus have not considered women of a childbearing age to be suitable for promotion at all. Promotions and careers do depend on a continuous programme of work in most instances and, like in Snakes and Ladders, a woman returning after childbirth can find herself several places back from where she left. Not all jobs are like this: medicine and dentistry, the law and the theatre all have the quality of not only being interruptable but also having the possibility of self-regulated hours of work. The Employment Protection Act provisions are thus an integral part of equality but they might have a drawback for white-collar unions.

In outline, the statutory provisions are as follows: if a woman has been working up to eleven weeks before the expected date of delivery and informs the employer of this date and of her intention to return to work and has been with her employer for two continuous years, she is then entitled to maternity leave. Paid maternity leave of six weeks of 90 per cent of her pay, less maternity allowance, will be obtainable as of right. A Maternity Pay Fund will make rebates to employers who have to make these payments. If an employer refuses to comply, the woman can take the matter up with an industrial tribunal which may order payment. In addition to this, a woman may return to work at her original, or comparable, job at any time up to twenty-nine weeks after confinement. This then provides the basis for a continuity of employment. Any employer who refuses to permit a return, or indeed attempts to pre-empt the whole situation by dismissing the employee because she is pregnant will be on the 'wrong end' of unfair dismissal procedures.

The problem for white-collar unions is that many maternity provision agreements have been negotiated at standards well above those above, in both the private and public sectors. Minimum standards in enactments such as this also tend to become the maxima and whilst this is a great step forward in areas where this form of agreement does not exist at all, it may actually stimulate industrial action in the white-collar fields. This is because employers will attempt to stick at the provisions in the Act whilst unions will try to get them to conform to the best practice. The pace-making Swedes provide for a year's leave which may be split between the mother and the father.

The maternity leave provisions are, however, still only a first step in providing a framework in which opportunities can be equalised for both men and women. The Sex Discrimination Act takes this matter somewhat further. The Act makes some forms of discrimination on the grounds of sex or marital status an offence. Much of the Act applies to non-work practice: mortgages, club memberships, etc., and these are welcome, too. It is necessary to define the three different types of discrimination which affect trade unions and especially non-manual unions.

Discrimination in education and in further education is the first and, in all probability, the most vital. With the best will in the world it is impossible for a union to argue for the preferment of women employees if they have neither the educational background nor the expertise to do the jobs concerned. We have noted earlier the small percentage of women in medicine, and the same applies to dentistry, and law, accountancy, engineering and almost every profession. A more balanced intake into the universities and the professional courses is necessary to remedy this. But the educational bias starts much earlier. Attitudes as to the roles the sexes will have in adult life are partly formed at schools and partly at home. Girls take subjects like domestic science and needlework, while boys practise woodwork, and this philosophy pervades the school system. Until attitudes change the Act is of only marginal value. If this form of discrimination ceases then it will be possible, when the present young children become parents themselves, to have a society with different attitudes. The time lag involved is nearer forty than thirty years.

The second discrimination is in the job placement. Advertisements now have to be unisex, and although this may be important in some cases it is still marginal. Until sufficient women have qualified to do the jobs advertised, men will get the jobs which they have become accustomed to getting as of right. Women, advertisements aside, will also be able to complain if they have been refused a job purely on the grounds of their sex.

The third, and obviously most immediate source of concern to unions, is the discrimination in employment. This can take the form of a bar to, or a limitation on, promotion prospects or it can be overt discrimination in the non-salary elements of the remuneration package; for example, refusing concessionary mortgages to women employees whilst providing them for men. Breaches of the Act in employment situations, including victimisation, may be referred to an industrial tribunal. The tribunal may, if the case is proved, award compensation and also make an order compelling the employer to comply with the provisions of the Act.

The Act also set up the Equal Opportunities Commission which has indefinite yet wide-ranging responsibilities. It can itself initiate action in tribunals and it can investigate or report on almost any issue. If the legislation works in the short term, this will mean more women being promoted and getting jobs in the white-collar sector. This may now help the unions – it did not in the past because women were far harder to recruit into unions than men, and are still more diffident about taking, and then sustaining, industrial action. But this, observably, is changing and opponents of that view argue that the Act will change it further. Ultimately this must be true. However, the attitudes which have led to this state of affairs will take longer to eradicate than the short-term benefits and the time lag could conceivably work against trade union growth or effectiveness. On moral grounds or more significantly, on grounds of equality the legislation is long overdue. On social grounds it may be some time before both men and women fully adjust to the new possibilities. On economic grounds it is a necessity – for too long the British have undervalued or wasted the potential of 50 per cent of the population. Unions will have to orientate themselves to represent their women members at industrial tribunals and to put pressure on employers to implement the Act whilst simultaneously being careful in watching for abuse. An example of this is the insurance company which decided that their lower two grades of staff could not get concessionary mortgages; strangely these grades comprised most of the women on the staff. In itself this sounds as though it is caught by the Act and is discriminatory. However, the company (one which negotiates only with a staff association) claims that the reason is that the salaries paid for these grades cannot be considered high enough to obtain a mortgage in the current state of the market. Meanwhile, the challenge has been thrown down and white-collar unions who fail to pick it up delay the enfranchisement of their female membership.

The Social Security Pensions Act which did not become fully operational until April 1978 is the latest in a series of legislative attempts to obtain a comprehensive state retirement pension system dating back to the aborted Crossman plan of 1970. White-collar unions are particularly affected but, for the purposes of this chapter, the interesting point is how this provides for the widening of negotiations. No employer was able to contract employees into or out of the proposed state second-tier arrangements without consultations at least three months in advance of the decision. This was a remarkable facility in that it is tantamount to a compulsion to negotiate. The whole Act has other useful provisions. Although white-collar unions have, over time, become more expert in pension negotiations and won notable victories, there are still a number of employers who refuse to negotiate on pension arrangements. The engineering industry contains a very high proportion of these.

The larger companies are multi-plant and if their plants are affiliates of the Association of Engineering Employers then each has separate negotiations and separate local procedure arrangements. Pensions, however, are normally still a central group-oriented matter, although some groups still run up to thirty different schemes. In the case of a single scheme the employers claim that there is no procedural provision for group-wide negotiations and everyone agrees that no one industrial plant's claim can be settled without all the other plants agreeing. This obstructionism, and it is nothing less than that, had to stop when the new legislation provoked companies into taking a look at their superannuation requirements.

The Health and Safety at Work etc. Act 1974 is very similar to the legislation prepared by the Conservative Government but which fell along with it in February 1974. It provides a framework for trade union activities and has to be viewed as enabling legislation which will only be as effective as those involved make it. The Act sets up the Health and Safety Commission and Executive which has the same sort of functional responsibilities as the Equal Opportunities Commission but which is also charged with publishing the codes of practice on which the Act's specific actions depend. Health and safety is often thought of simply in the most dramatic terms, that is affecting coal miners, trawlermen, machine operators and agricultural workers with little or no publicity given to hazards facing the white-collar employees. These, however, are substantial and in some cases even lethal though admittedly, offices tend to be safer places in which to work than factories or building sites. Few, if any, typists, addressographists or collators have suffered an industrial injury from their machines. There are, nevertheless, great health hazards for the growing numbers of technical personnel. Chemicals are now being used in manufacturing processes without any detailed knowledge of their medium-term effects on an individual, let alone the long-term health hazards; PVC is one case that has come to light; but how many have not? Infectious hepatitis presents a grave (sometimes fatal, most often disabling and always uncomfortable) risk in all branches of medicine and dentistry, including the laboratory and nursing staffs. Laboratories can be death traps because of inadequate equipment, bad lay-out and poor precautionary techniques. The Act, though considerably weakened by the words 'as far as is reasonably practicable' scattered like confetti amongst the sections, does provide a chance for unions to have an impact in the area.

Manual workers' unions, notably in mining, shipping, textiles and railways, have always made strenuous efforts to combat physical exploitation and quite successfully. However, up to the advent of this legislation the legal position and the moral climate was for compensation after the event rather than for prevention. Technological advances have outstripped our knowledge of effects and this is where the unions will be important. The Act provides for the appointment of safety representatives or stewards and if required by the employees, a safety committee. The committees will be multi-union with both manual and white-collar together. The representatives there will negotiate with management on matters which will be delineated in a health and safety procedure agreement. There will thus be a three-way union approach. Through direct negotiations at plant or enterprise level, through the inter-union committee system and then through the health and safety commission, its codes and regulations, prohibition notices issued by the factory inspectorate and with the Employment Advisory Service. This will all need expertise and unions are finding it necessary to appoint full-time safety officers. Once again, the range and scope of collective bargaining is being increased.

Some white-collar union members may, however, have a unique problem, as well as the union itself. The Act stipulates that managements have the prime responsibility for health and safety matters, yet unions such as ASTMS, TASS, the EMA, POMSA, etc., have managers in membership. There may well be cases, unfortunate but true, when trade union members are both culpable and liable to prosecution, even down to assistant supervisor and chargehand grades. The union may also have a problem. A safety committee may ask for an investigation into an incident and the committee finds that a foreman ASTMS member has been negligent – ASTMS members are on this committee. The professional official may well be called in to defend the member and he or she will be placed in a difficult position of challenging another member's evidence in an industrial situation. Whilst this probably will not often occur, it has at least once to date. The matter was resolved and the law prevailed, but it could lead to awkward situations.

One matter that white-collar unions will want the Employment Medical Advisory Service to investigate is the very difficult one of stress at work. Stress is unfortunately a very over-used and misused term and problems abound on this subject. What is stress, how does it differ from strain, if at all? Does it have to have physical manifestations, such as the case of a psychosomatic disease? What causes stress? How does one isolate stress in the work environment from that created in the home environment? These are just some of the more basic difficulties.

It is, however, a singularly important subject. There is little doubt in the minds of most occupational medicine workers that stress does exist and does do damage. It can exist because the job is too boring or because it is too demanding. It may be that the workplace is too dangerous or silent, there may be too much contact with fellow employees, or too little. The boredom and alienation arguments are as well known as are the Institute of Directors' studies on stress and very senior management. What the white-collar unions are interested in are the middle-ranked employees.

Studies in the US suggest that the most pressured and stressed of all employees are those in first- and second-line supervisory jobs. The reasoning is that these employees have to exercise their authority directly on the shop-floor worker, which in itself is a pressure position, but at the same time are themselves under pressure from management. They are seen as management by the shop floor and as an extension of the shop floor by management. They are thus caught in a squeeze and the US evidence is that this group of employees exhibit a consistently higher percentage of what are thought to be stress diseases than any other group. Other employees, doctors and managers especially have to work under considerable mental pressure in that a mistake can cost lives or cost jobs and one suspects that stress is a problem. The matter, however, can be summed up in the view that one man's stress is another man's challenge.

Both in the approach to stress and the whole area of health and safety, the white-collar employees can play a vital role. This is often highlighted by the health and safety officers in membership, along with members who have a very high degree of technical and specialised knowledge about diseases, chemicals, processes and substances. This information source is waiting to be trapped for the benefit of all employees, and will probably be brought about by TUC initiative.

The Industry Act, 1975 is yet another new piece of legislation which may, but only may, affect trade unions in a specific sense. The Act will have, if fully used, a great part to play in the restructuring of British industry and therefore the securing and future of people's jobs. There are, however, two separate sections in the Act; the disclosure of information provisions and the planning agreements proposals which may have far-reaching effects.

The information in question is very different from that which will be provided under the Employment Protection Act. The type of information in this instance is less concerned with immediacy of negotiating and more with the long-term problems of the future of the enterprise. One great disappointment is that the provisions apply only to companies in the manufacturing sector. The provisions were considerably watered down in the Act's passage and the union involvement is now really an afterthought given that information has to be provided to the Secretary of State. The tragedy here from the trade union point of view is that at one time it appeared that there would be at least a right to information.

Employees have always been in an inferior role in Britain where information is concerned. The best way for most personnel or their unions to find out what is happening is to read the financial press. Naturally, this is most unsatisfactory. Managements expect loyalty and hard work from their staffs, but when they do not let them know what the future of the company is, whether it is trying to expand or contract, then that loyalty is at risk. It then becomes a gamble for a man or woman to change jobs, for this has to be done without proper information on which to base a rational decision.

The information is to be made available to an 'authorised representative' or a 'relevant' trade union. Companies may be tempted to choose the most complaint union they can trace and provide its representative with the information and, by playing on the commercial secrecy conditions, hope that the information will not get past that one man. Whether or not information is provided to a union is dependent upon the discretion of the Secretary of State who, for reasons of national security or 'special reason', will refuse to do so. An advisory committee will adjudicate on matters in dispute concerning the furnishing of information and at this point the union can defend its interest. The information will be concerned with the undertaking's capital expenditure and its acquisition or disposal, output and productivity, sales, exports, research and development and manpower. To date no information orders have been laid by the Secretary of State so that there is no conceptual framework yet for either the details which will be made available or the Secretary of State's interpretation of the factors involved in the 'special reasons'.

The second potentially important point concerns planning agreements. This is potentially because agreements are to be wholly voluntary and as a result the system may not be comprehensive enough. It is unfortunate that the information provisions became weakened in concept; it is a tragedy that planning agreements have not been used to fulfil their potential. The original idea was that the appropriate government department and a company would, after consultations with the unions involved, reach an agreement. This would, in a sense, be a rolling corporate plan and the government could, if it wished, by judicious use of investment grants, loans or by other means, channel production into the areas which it considered to be of social or special commercial importance. These would include the stimulation of production for export, or for import substitutes, regional employment policy, environmental and resource depletion considerations amongst many others. It would also have provided government with that early disaggregated information without which it cannot plan ahead effectively.

From the trade union point of view the planning agreement was (or perhaps still is) the first time that employees have had the chance to be involved in forward planning procedures instead of always having to react to given events. It is obviously far better for trade union members to realise that the probable manpower requirements in a specific company will be reduced by X per cent in three years' time rather than have the ninety-days' notice. In the former case the union and management can sit down to work out a strategy of gradual run down; in the latter, the union has more time in which to pursue its normal reactive function. Needless to say, the first method is by far the most preferable. It is doubly so when it is in the context of an agreement which explains investment intentions, productivity considerations and market analyses. Trade unionists are rightly suspicious of many of the statements made by companies in redundancy situations: far too many times a company has been on the brink of disaster yet apparently returned record profits. The planning agreement is a method for allaying these suspicions. It is also the ideal vehicle for taking industrial democracy to shop-floor level rather than allowing it to develop at board level only.

Most of the companies which might be candidates for planning agreements are multi-plant, multi-product and probably multi-national. They would also have many unions (both white-collar and manual) with negotiating rights. As a result, the mechanisms needed for consultations at plant, division and group levels will be complex. It will also mean a duplication of effort amongst unions unless arrangements are made on a group basis or a national research centre is set up. If the trade unions are to avoid becoming mere information receivers, they must arrange for both the education of the members and the full-time officials and for a huge expansion of their research facilities. To question effectively one must understand and to do this one must always get behind the facts as presented and dig into the premises on which they are based. Unions like ASTMS can direct their educatonal facilities towards this, but in the event are in a better position than other private-sector unions. This is because their memberships often have a significant percentage of employees in middle and senior management who can understand and explain the techniques used; enough scientists to verify (or otherwise) optimism about research and enough marketing people to do the same about projections.

The planning agreement concept did, however, fall into some disrepute in the wake of the take-over by Peugeot-Citroen of Chrysler UK. Chrysler was the only company which had negotiated a planning agreement with the government and at the time of the take-over was just putting the finishing touches to its second-year plan. Despite the statements of interest in the agreement neither the government nor the unions knew of the impending take-over. Not unnaturally, this has caused the unions to re-evaluate the system and they are now thinking in terms of loyally binding agreements.

This whole package of legislation is bound to change traditional trade union habits. Collective bargaining will be on a wider basis than ever before and participation will be greater than before. To the new advantages there are corresponding responsibilities. Commercial secrecy must be observed and agreements must be honoured. Care will have to be taken that the unions are not absorbed into the corporate structure and that their traditional functions are not compromised. Members and full-time officials will need to know more and be more accurate than ever before because mistakes will bring with them far greater losses for the membership. White-collar unions with the technical and managerial expertise at their elbows should be well placed to take maximum advantage of the new situation.

It will probably be at least five years before the full benefits are realised or even the full implications of this legislative revolution digested. By then the legislation may have been joined by that on industrial democracy and we shall deal with this in chapter 9.

Chapter 8

Incomes policies

'Annual income twenty pounds, annual expenditure twenty pounds ought and six, result misery.' – Dickens

      ⌐ MᴀᴄCᴏʀʙᴇʀɪsᴍ !

From the Emperor Diocletian onwards there have been attempts at various forms of incomes policies: governments attempting to interpose themselves between an employer and an employee on the matter of the employee's wages. Since these times there have been few dissenting employers (initially at least), but also relatively few assenting employees. However, the incomes-policy strategy has come into its own since the Second World War with a proven record of non-success. We are not really referring to governments backing employers in their stand against trade unions in, for example, the 1926–31 era, we are referring to policies to which some form of government constraint has been applied, or to which the government, as an employer can exert its own pressure.

Whilst it would be fascinating to chronicle the earlier attempts at incomes policies and their sanctions, for example, one such policy in Britain made it a felony to receive a wage above the norm and a felony to be unemployed (the Catch 22 of the thirteenth century), we shall concentrate instead on the post-war period, especially the 1960s and 1970s, and look at types of policy and the results of those policies.

There are, however, some general observations which should be made at this point. Despite repeated attempts to curtail the growth of incomes and despite the protestations that 'this will be the panacea', Britain now has high unemployment, a high rate of inflation and a shrinking industrial base; Britain is now one of the lowest wage economies in Europe – it has also one of the lowest industrial investment rates in Europe.

Why, then, as one policy followed another, has there been this keenness to repeat the same mistakes? Why should incomes be controlled yet the market mechanisms in other parts of the economy remain relatively unscathed? The answers are probably to be found by looking at the type of economic system in which we live and work and, because

policy. They also had a large (and rare) balance-of-payments surplus to aid them. However, by 1972, the terms of trade turned against Britain and with both inflation and the balance-of-payments deficit increasing, talks opened on a voluntary incomes policy.

It is worth noting at this point that the 1971 Industrial Relations Act had totally soured the relationship between the government and unions. Equally the Barber 'dash for growth' was basically encouraging asset stripping, the fringe banks and the property market both priced houses out of the reach of all but the better off, whilst many office blocks were built to stand empty. It would have been surprising if a voluntary system had succeeded; in fact it never got off the ground.

By November 1972 the government imposed a ninety-day freeze on all wage and salary increases with legal penalties and sanctions against those who broke the rules. This was followed by Phase II which established the Pay Board and a separate Price Commission (at least the previous attempt acknowledged their interdependence) and set a maximum pay increase of £1 plus 4 per cent.

One very irritating feature of this period for the authors was that ASTMS had prepared an internal document which detailed the anomalies and described the loopholes in the White Paper. It was leaked and published and, subsequently, every single loophole was closed. Phase II opened a completely new era of statutory policy – complexity. The do's and don't's were detailed, and i's dotted, and t's crossed and consequently no loopholes seemed left. The result was that small employers circumnavigated the policy, new techniques aided high settlements and unions took industrial action on the 'special cases' provided for. A one-day national strike (the first since 1926) took place on 1 May.

In 1973 the price of oil quintupled. The government, faced with higher costs across industry and commerce, and a gigantic balance-of-payments deficit, announced Phase III. Phase III was continued with a maximum increase – this time 7 per cent (up to £350 per year) or £2·25 per week, and threshold payments which triggered after a 7 per cent increase in the Retail Price Index and on every per-cent rise subsequently. Interestingly, this was premised on a Treasury assumption of falling commodity prices – an incomprehensible error which could only be explained by malevolence. The policy also reintroduced productivity deals, although the criteria were such that to the authors' knowledge no one company had an internal accounting system capable of monitoring it. The TUC opposed Phase III, as they did Phases I and II.

In December 1973 the government placed the country on a three-day week in response to the miners' claim in excess of the statutory norm and the associated industrial action. February 1974 saw the miners' strike and an 'Anomalies Commission' paper being prepared on the claim. However, the government decided to hold on, and eventually a

Labour Government was returned. Yet again, incomes policy had brought down a government. Little can be learned from this policy. The underlying political factors doomed it to failure from the outset, the main surprise being that it lasted so long.

The Labour Government announced, as had the Conservatives, that there would be no statutory incomes policies – only the 'Social Contract'. This had been forged by the alliance created by adversity between the Labour Party and the unions, repairing all the ravages created during the lives of the 1964–70 governments. Phase III was abolished in July 1974 although it had virtually been inoperative, other than threshold payments, since the election. The TUC drew up a list of points to be followed by negotiators and in return a list of policies to be followed by the government, including the Employment Protection Act and the Industry Act, was promised. The idea was that earnings should rise by no more than the Retail Price Index increases.

However, a combination of a catch-up following Phase III and consolidation of all the thresholds gave rise to increases of 30 per cent and more, whilst inflation rose and the pound fell. Although many of these large increases contained a large element of 'old money', that is the consolidation of thresholds and other items into basic salary thus increasing only the wage drift element, there was panic. Yet again the entire weight of the media blamed inflation almost exclusively on earnings and consistently forgot the deliberate Budget stimulation of indirect tax increases, public utility price increases, and above all, the depreciation of the pound increasing all import costs.

In July 1975, a voluntary £6 across-the-board increase was introduced, described by a white-collar union general secretary (Ken Gill of TASS) as 'voluntary as rape', it was a most ingenious policy. An Act, the Grants Charges and Remuneration Act, was rushed through the House; this allowed, amongst other things, an employer to breach a contract of employment if payments exceeded those laid down in the White Paper. It also provided that employers who paid more than the limit would not be allowed *any* price increase by the Price Commission. Dividends were restrained and prices constrained. The £6 was a supplement, counting for pension purposes only and a maximum, but those earning £8,500 or over per year, received no increase. Incremental schemes, providing they were self-financing, job re-structuring and productivity scheme payments, both provided they were already in existence, were allowed to be paid.

The plan (Phase I) was remarkably successful. It had the backing of the TUC and most unions and, indeed, awarded increases of a far greater percentage than many low-paid union members had received before. It also, however, distorted differential patterns, a matter of great concern to all white-collar unions. It was clear from the outset that this incomes policy would have to last for at least three years. It was equally obvious that unemployment would continue to rise and the pound would continue to fall.

In April 1976, the Chancellor, Denis Healey, announced tax cuts in his Budget – conditional upon the acceptance of Phase II. This most important step was a milestone in corporate-state-style collective bargaining and in June 1976, a TUC Special Congress overwhelmingly accepted the concept. Phase II was a trifle more complex than Phase I. It had a 5 per cent increase with an upper limit of £4 and a lower limit of £2·50 per week, again as a supplement to income. Inflation continued to rise – real disposable earnings began to fall. If ever the lie has been given to the idea that earnings are the major component of inflation, it was this period. Average earnings rose 8 per cent year on year, whilst inflation rose 16 per cent. By April 1977, some people's living standards had fallen by nearly 30 per cent over two years and these were people well within the collective-bargaining orbit.

Although the Chancellor attempted to make another trade-off between income-tax cuts and wage increases, the new attempt was doomed to failure. Instead the TUC stuck to its 1977 Autumn Congress decision of 'an orderly return to free collective bargaining'. Orderly in this instance meant observance of the twelve-month gap between major settlements. The new Prices Bill re-enacted the Grants Charges and Remuneration Act, but the White Paper, which was the heart of the policy, specifically stated that only the 'twelve-month rule' was statutory – the rest of the document which asked for increases in *earnings* to be kept under 10 per cent was merely a statement of policy.

The government however had control of the public sector purse strings through 'cash limits' and direct and indirect payments. In the private sector the government started to apply sanctions and threats through its procurement policy and its discretionary-payments policy. At the time of writing these have not yet been fully tested in the courts, although two white-collar unions, ASTMS and IPCS, intend to so so if necessary. Examples of private-sector interference were the removal of the Export Credit Guarantee loan to William Mackies of Belfast, who nevertheless completed their order satisfactorily, and the blacklisting of other companies, generally small, but including the John Lewis Partnership. An attempt to use legal action against the Sun Alliance Insurance Company foundered as it was *ultra vires*, as was attempted interference in the Industrial Training Board Settlements. A new weapon of government contract undertakings has now been added to this armoury but, as with the previous systems, only small firms have been 'picked-off'. Self-financing productivity schemes came back into vogue at this point in time. To all intents and purposes, the incomes policy was terminally sick, if not clinically dead. Providing the DoE was kept at barge-pole length and negotiations conducted quietly and efficiently, union members could start to catch up on their previous losses.

1978 saw Phase IV of the policy and a totally contradictory and confused state of affairs. The August White Paper let all statutory regulations fall into abeyance but contained a 5 per cent pay limit to be enforced by cash limits in the public sector and sometimes in the private sector, the same recipe as for 1977. This policy was rejected both by the TUC Congress and the Labour Party Conference. It was clear from the outset that the trade union movement felt that this figure was far too low. The Ford workers rejected a 15 per cent offer, an offer which the company frankly stated was made only because of the government policy. The ensuing nine-week dispute ended with a total settlement in the region of 18 per cent, of which 9·5 per cent was applied to the basic rate. Whilst this clearly broke the incomes policy it was also apparent that the Ford profit and their ability to pay the increases played a considerable part in the final settlement. The private sector was thus bound to have varying levels of claims and settlements dependent upon profits.

The government imposed sanctions on Ford by refusing to buy new cars from them and were then defeated in a House of Commons vote directly on this subject. The major problem for this phase of incomes policy is however, at the time of writing, almost certain to be in the public sector with the local authority workers and miners in the forefront. Productivity schemes and other payments which can remove much of the heat in the private sector are often inappropriate or unworkable in the public sector and without this safety valve little hope can be held out for a dispute-free period.

What then had this round of incomes policies taught us? First, the policies were effective because they were so ill-defined and because of TUC backing. The fact that the Department of Employment had total control over what could, or could not, be paid and the fact that the guidelines they worked to were never published, made it an easy policy to control. Equally the DoE did not allow precedent to be a factor in deciding on the merits of a case. It became clear from the very outset that if we were subject to regulations which we did not know (a Kafkaesque situation) then the Department had to be avoided at all costs. No union could find a loophole (because no barrier existed) only an invisible force field.

The policy failed because the trade union leadership could not guarantee continuing control over its members. Although most large manual unions supported incomes policy, the overwhelming majority of white-collar unions did not and they proved not only to be the catalyst but also a significant proportion of the opposition. Differentials had been decimated over the years; real disposable incomes savagely cut – along with the 'social wage'. Anomalies abounded, promotions were frustrated and intra-enterprise productivity fell. One most disturbing fact was at the 1977 TUC Congress, when a leader from a large union proclaimed that in free collective bargaining, the lions got the lion's share. Looked at objectively what he meant was that we should never have free collective bargaining again, only an administered incomes policy. Fortunately the overwhelming majority of trade union members disagreed and they made this plain. The last six months of Phase II was punctuated by unofficial dispute actions taken by the skilled workers whose differentials over the unskilled had all but disappeared. Phase III was a signal for even more dispute action as union members, often in defiance of their Executive's advice, sought to regain their living standards. Many of these disputes were in the white-collar sector, a notable one being the CPSA air traffic control assistants' strike in Autumn 1977.

These incomes policies have had two distinct impacts. One is on negotiations and the other is on the attitudes of white-collar employees and their unions. Negotiations in all of these periods were frequently unreal. Unions and employers negotiated knowing full well that in many of the cases the only argument was whether they agreed on the maximum, allowable, amount. Employers often apologised for being unable to settle at higher levels and assured the unions that, but for Government policy, they would have behaved differently. Some meant it. It is interesting to note that after each policy, both the social partners set their faces against another nationally imposed incomes policy.

There were, however, also individual problems in each policy which characterised it and also directed the conduct of negotiations, sometimes leaving a later problem, sometimes starting a new trend. The 1967 policy was characterised by its preoccupation with productivity bargaining and, as we saw in an earlier chapter, this was adopted by the white-collar unions and continues today. The Phases II and III policies left open the negotiation of pensions schemes and stimulated union interest in trust funds. The overall trade union preoccupation with occupational pensions schemes and the militancy shown by members in negotiations stems from this date. The policy also had to come to grips with London weighting allowances and these not only re-emerged as a bargaining issue, but more usefully in the long term, an index was constructed and published in the *Department of Employment Gazette*.

The £6 limit policy was, in practice, the most rigorous. Pension-scheme bargaining, except for the occasions when this had started before the incomes policy was introduced, was not allowed and new productivity bargaining effectively ceased. From the white-collar staffs' point of view the only favourable feature was the protection of their incremental scales due to the fierce opposition to interference mounted by the civil servants. Not every increment was paid everywhere and this is the first time that increments have been attacked in this fashion; other incomes policies left them as a balancing factor against the overtime and shift-pay element in manual-workers' salaries. The White Paper stated that increments could be paid providing that they were self-funding. Both the Civil Service and local government authorities certified this was the case in their spheres, but not only has there been no check on this, all the evidence is that this was not universal in local government and that the national authorities realised it. Nevertheless, full increments were paid in the public service. In the private sector, however, many large companies were then told by the DoE that they must prove self-financing; some could not and thus there was a shortfall in expected increases.

The 1976 policy very slightly opened the differentials concertina, but the problems of 're-entry' grew more formidable. The upshot of this was a rapidly increasing militancy amongst these members, and a steady stream of applicants to white-collar unions. Once again differentials *and* purchasing power were being eroded. This is part of the second impact of incomes policies. White-collar workers believe, and as we have demonstrated, they are statistically correct, that they are the principal casualties. Since 1966, the only full year without an incomes policy of any description was 1971. The economic results of this dozen years of restriction can hardly be looked upon as a good advertisement for such policies. However, white-collar union recruitment has never been higher. In the engineering industry, ASTMS increased its membership by over 70 per cent within three years, despite it being an industry in which it was already entrenched. If there is any single factor which stimulates white-collar union growth, it is government-imposed incomes policy.

From a government's point of view, the sad thing about incomes policies is that they have to end. Although it cannot be pretended that there are no anomalies in the British remuneration structure, it does reflect to some degree the skills, qualifications, responsibilities, availabilities and efforts in the labour market. Whatever the form of incomes policy, it has to have a distorting effect on this market on the relative rates of pay and in the longer run, relative job attraction and recruitment. Equally, whatever the policy, some groups will be disadvantaged and no policy is flexible enough to deal with this. The 1966–70 policies attempted to have exemptions for special cases, but in turn these spawned more resentment and distorted relativities. Unless incomes are always centrally administered in a corporate-state condition, then free collective bargaining must return. Central administration of wages and salaries on a permanent basis would argue that there must also be a direction of labour and a totalitarian regime to impose it, because otherwise the distortions in the labour market would literally make the British economy unworkable. Fortunately we are far from such a situation. But the unions have a responsibility to ensure that these incomes policies have a finite life, and the shorter the better.

Governments wish them to continue because they realise that when they end, the catch-up process starts all over again. That is why employees join unions in larger numbers in the periods of incomes policy. The 1970/2 and 1974/5 earnings increases were merely a re-establishment of previously held positions. Surely unions are about, indeed political economic systems are about, improving living standards, not worsening them, and thus allowing a mass scramble to catch up, before worsening them again.

Incomes policies have thus foundered, on a regular basis, for similar reasons and all have been introduced for a similar reason – a crisis situation. The policies have all been designed to cope with short-term problems and have thus been short-term expedients so it should be no surprise that they generate pressures which cause them to collapse. We have never in Britain tried to get a long-term incomes policy of any description.

A paper by NIESR, a body previously noted for its advocacy of incomes policy, suggests that those tried since the war have not worked – there has always been a catch-up. It also points out that whilst real incomes are reduced quickly the catch-up takes longer, often two years. If incomes policies have not been successful in themselves, then in broader, economic terms they have been counter-productive. They militate against investment because expectations of probable demand are low and uncertain. This in turn has reduced output, helped to swell imports and brought the next incomes policy inexorably nearer.

It is surely clear that incomes are only one factor in a whole bundle of economic parameters which need planning. To single out incomes is to take a palliative measure whilst leaving the underlying disease un-treated. If governments wish to have incomes policies then they must be set firmly in the long-term planning of the economy with the other factors given at least equal weight and equal statutory sanctions. We are not advocating such a policy, merely pointing out that it is an essential pre-condition for any long-lasting incomes policy. Surely though we have seen the last of short-term incomes policies, looked at rationally they just don't work – and never will in a free democratic society for any considerable length of time. The argument must be this: if the market is basically allowed to work in all other respects, why not for an employee's labour too?

Unions and their officers have a great deal of expertise in the collective-bargaining arena but it is, however, only a part of the role of trade unions. One other objective is to demand participation in the decision-making processes at the workplace. This can be met in various ways and we discuss these in the next chapter.

Chapter 9

The widening of traditional horizons

'I don't want to belong to any club that will accept me as a member.' –
Groucho Marx

The salariat is deeply concerned with its remuneration, its power and its
place in the social strata but is reacting differently in each of the industrialised countries. In the past its recourse would have been to a political
party, now it is to industrial organisation.

Countries develop at rates and in ways which seem to have a momentum of their own and defy predictions and laws. Some countries
industrialised before others, some retained the feudal system longer,
indeed still retain it, some are capitalist, some socialist, many are a
mixture of these. Their industrial relations are all different in form and
style. The approaches to the relationship between those who work and
those who employ differ very fundamentally. In some instances,
Germany and the United States (for example) there is the underlying
belief that employees should identify with the employer and work
harmoniously together, although certainly in the US this relationship is
punctuated by painful and often violent industrial actions. In France,
there are four union centres: the CGT is basically communist; another,
the CFDT, is socialist; a third is non-confessional catholic, and finally
there is a white-collar-only centre, the FO. In Britain there is a halfway-
house position, but the conflict instinct is still lively.

Of all the countries so far mentioned, Britain has by far the most
developed white-collar union sector. Indeed, apart from the USA it has
the highest percentage of white-collar workers in the labour force. But
the Scandinavians have higher union penetrations: in Sweden, very
senior civil servants, police officers, public prosecutors and judges are
all members of trade unions as a matter of course. Britain, with its large
number of trade unionists, its large number of white-collar workers and
its propensity to direct conflict situations is trying at present to work
out its own solution. The ACAS is the first serious and formal attempt
to channel conflict into the arbitration room generally accepted by
parliament, unions and employers. But it has come into existence as a

series of controversial incomes policies which have cut middle-class purchasing power at a time when that group is becoming unionised.

Britain has staggered from economic crisis to economic crisis since 1945. In the recent past, these crises have basically been caused by the balance-of-payments deficits and the need to defend sterling; the traditional remedy has been to slow down the economy by deflating it, thus creating the stop-go cycle. The balance of payments problem has been compounded by high rates of inflation since 1970, to the extent that the term 'stagflation' has become an unpleasant reality. Every time there has been a stop in the cycle, investment stopped too. What has made matters worse is that the governments of the day have invariably got their timing wrong, so that Britain deflated after we had reached the peak and inflated half-way up an upsurge. The result of this is the well known run-down in manufacturing capital, although there are even more reasons which go to explain this failure. So Britain has been badly placed to withstand inflation as the chances of getting the increased productivity to absorb some of it are decreased because of out-dated machinery. By 1972 it had become fashionable to blame inflation on the trade union movement, ignoring all the external components and indeed, other institutionalised, internal causes.

This specific change was not entirely new as we saw in the previous chapter. It was really the manifestation of the decline of British power, of the economy and of a manifest inability to control it. A scapegoat was needed and the unions were unkindly and most unjustly volunteered. The result was the most detailed and complex incomes policy yet devised and the Industrial Relations Act.

This period was crucial. Trade union members did not believe that they were responsible for all of the nation's shortcomings. They resented the allegations especially as they were being made by those that they considered were more culpable than themselves. It was clear that there had been a failure of management at all levels and in all sectors. When the property boom, the asset strippers and the conglomerates came along in the early 1970s, the cynicism turned to anger and from the anger came positive proposals. The newly returned Labour Government produced much legislation conferring affirmative rights on trade unions. In trade union circles, however, the discussions were also centralised around industrial democracy, participation or control. If management had failed then surely trade unionists could make a better fist of it went one argument; another was that Britain is a democratic country, yet this democracy ceases the moment employees enter the work place – surely this is wrong; yet others linked workers' control with the overtones of capitalism.

Our accession into the EEC had stimulated much of the argument. The Fifth Directive, and its subsequent amendments, means that market

members have to have a measure of industrial democracy. Being a
Directive, this is binding only as to the ends, not the means so that
many types of possible legislation were being discussed. This Directive
has been in draft form for many years, a fact which shows the great
difficulties involved in the subject and at present the draft involves the
German-style two-tier board system. The German method, using
management and supervisory boards was rooted in a works committee
system. This system grew out of weak trade unions and is virtually unknown in Britain. The Dutch system was similarly unfamiliar and
probably unexportable. The Danes and Swedes both had industrial
democracy systems linked with progressive employee ownership of
enterprises – a system which would be unworkable given the large
institutional stock and share holdings in Britain.

These factors of continually recurring crises, EEC entry and other
countries' apparent advantages stimulated the discussion, a discussion
which is of particular significance to white-collar workers, especially
managers. In essence it is a debate on the future running of the country
and, interestingly, one which continues at a time when Britain has new
advantages over the medium term. North Sea oil, with its relief on the
balance of payments and its large resources accruing mainly to the
public sector, could prove to have an immense positive stimulus.

In many ways, the extension of industrial democracy is an objective
implicit in the notion of trade unionism itself. A vital theme running
through many recent developments in collective bargaining has been the
insistence by trade unionists on transferring to the realm joint regula-
tion issues which had previously been regarded as belonging to the area
of unilateral managerial authority. The boundaries of managerial auto-
nomy are constantly being eroded, as the extent of what is accepted as
'management's right to manage' becomes narrower. The increasing
importance of the *status quo* clause, the decentralisation of bargaining,
and the 'shop stewards' movement' which both stimulated and fed off
that process are, in different ways, examples of how these developments
have worked in practice. The white-collar movement has mirrored this
process and in some ways is giving it a push forward.

These kinds of responses are not peculiar to the UK; the problem
which engendered them is common, in varying ways, to all industrial
nations. Widespread acknowledgment that a problem exists has created
an acceptance by both sides of industry, and not just in this country, that
the industrial structure of the developed countries needs re-examining.
In the Scandinavian countries, for example, there have been attempts to
change the structure and content of work itself, by replacing production-
line techniques and the monotony and frustration they inevitably
create, with 'autonomous work groups', where small teams build complete products, with a considerable degree of control over the way the

work is performed. These reforms are harder to execute for groups of routine office workers who now seem to be exhibiting the same symptoms of alienation.

All of these developments are different kinds of response to the same general range of problems. The idea of industrial democracy itself is, of course, not new; but the resurgence of the debate about it – whether as 'participation', or at the other extreme, workers' control – is indicative of the ways in which current industrial technology and structure have rendered the old patterns of control and work relationships both obsolete and unacceptable.

This is just as important in the new 'factories' created by the introduction of office machinery and data-retrieval. The Sudreau Report on industrial democracy in France commented upon a 'contradiction' between the current demands of industrial technology and the abilities and aspirations produced by increasingly sophisticated levels of education; the more highly educated the workforce becomes, the more routine and mechanical are the tasks it is called upon to perform. Finally, and in many ways linked with these other factors, there is the physical size of companies.

What is often described as the 'logic' of industrial production has led in recent years to a growing concentration of industry, and a concomitant increase in the size of companies. The extent to which this has occurred in British industry is demonstrated in Table 9.1.

TABLE 9.1

Share of largest firms in net output (%)	1935	1958	1963	1968
50 firms	14·9	24·7	27·3	32·4
100 firms	24·0	32·2	37·4	42·0
200 firms	NA	41·0	47·9	52·5
Share of largest firms in employment (%)				
50 firms	15·0	21·2	24·3	29·4
100 firms	22·0	27·7	32·6	37·8
200 firms	28·0	35·5	42·0	47·1

The results of this increasing concentration are well known. But less appreciated is the growing size of the clerical group or the research team where work is becoming increasingly collectivised. The employee of the giant corporation feels no sense of commitment to an organisation too big for him to identify with; decisions which affect him reach him from remote head offices, often in another continent, and are quite outside his control or even influence. The effect is disaffection, boredom, frustration, or what the sociologists have summarised as alienation.

It is against this background that the debate on worker directors has taken place, and while there is probably a high degree of consensus within the British trade union movement about the general analysis, there is far less agreement about either the desirability or relevance of worker directors as remedies. This absence of agreement is partly to do with the novelty of the idea in the British context, and the complexity and variety of the argument, but also because the white-collar worker seems readier than others to become involved in management.

The worker-director system embracing trade unionists under the right circumstances and on the right terms, may be a step in the right direction. We certainly do not think the appointment of worker directors will solve all the problems we have described so far; but we believe that these problems cannot properly be tackled without some sort of change in the current system of directorial appointment and control. The sine-cure directorship and 'political' appointment system are outmoded, and tend to inhibit change. British companies are run by an oligarchical, self-perpetuating process which guarantees the appointment of like-minded individuals, a process justified by neither equity nor performance. Apart from anything else, the introduction of worker directors could be a mechanism to hasten the decline of the co-optive, networked oligarchy, and to bring some fresh ideas to British boardrooms. Above all else, however, if white-collar worker directors with others are to succeed at any level, they must be introduced in a way that represents a genuine extension of industrial democracy, and not just its shadow. They are, however, only one form of industrial democracy, or more probably, a part of the process – not the whole.

It may be useful at this point to examine in a little detail the City Company Law Committee's First Report, as this provides a clear example of what we mean. It begins by stating, quite unequivocally, that the main concern is with an 'efficient and profitable private sector', and that they have examined employee participation in this light. It goes on to say that it may be the case that

> better communcation and a greater degree of participation by
> employees in the management of the company can lead to an
> increased commitment to the company's objectives, a recognition of
> the importance of ensuring its continuing profitability and an
> improvement in industrial relations.

There is no suggestion that they are interested in employee participation for its own sake; or even in employee participation as such. They regard the company's objectives as determined and final, and the only problem, therefore, is how best to promote them: the employee representatives are clearly not expected to shape or influence those objectives. This is unlikely to satisfy the salaried staffs.

The most vigorous white-collar union dissenters argue that the principal objective in creating a worker-director system is – precisely as the phrase 'industrial democracy' suggests – to make industry more democratic. In practical terms, we see it as a way of providing those who work in industry not simply with involvement in, but influence over decisions which vitally affect their lives: and that must include the power to actually alter those decisions where necessary. We believe workers have an absolute right to a voice in two crucial areas: the allocation of resources within the company, including manpower, plant and capital investment; and in the appointment of senior personnel, the quality of whose decisions directly affects their jobs. The effective exercise of that right requires more than a system in which worker directors are party to the decisions that would have been reached in their absence anyway: they must be capable of effectively altering them.

The clear implication here is that in certain cases at least, the presence of union directors will produce decisions different from those that would have been made without them. In its turn that implies a conflict of interest between staff and shareholders' representatives. The obvious example in which such conflict might be manifest is, of course, in the closure of a plant but there are others, including for example, the direction of new investment. In a sense, the notion of worker directors implies a difference in preoccupation and interest from ordinary directors. They will have their own real constituency which will actively question and monitor their activities.

An argument advanced by opponents of representation is that it would have an adverse effect on company efficiency. The EEC appear to endorse this view, for in the report already referred to, they say:

> it must be admitted that the problem of efficiency may become more acute if employee participation is organised in a way which permits the employees' representatives unilaterally to block the implementation of major economic decisions.

We find this line of argument objectionable in a number of ways. In the first place, we reject the suggestion that it will necessarily be employee representatives who stand in the way of sensible 'major economic decisions'.

It is generally accepted that the principal cause of Britain's recent poor industrial performance lies in the refusal of companies (and others) to invest sufficient capital in manufacturing industry. We can foresee circumstances where the union directors on a board are seeking to institute a substantial programme of direct industrial investment, but find their plans 'unilaterally' blocked by the shareholders' representatives. This would seem to us to carry implications for 'the problem of efficiency' to say nothing of the national interest. The salariat, where in unions, are showing signs of dissatisfaction.

We have argued that if worker directors are to represent a real extension of industrial democracy, they must have the power genuinely to influence and to alter decisions made at board level. We believe this to be a condition of trade union acceptance and indeed of employees' acceptance generally. We see no way that employees could be expected to develop any great trust or belief in a system in which their representatives were in a permanent minority, but it would be a start and, given the growth of salaried union membership, has a quality of inevitability.

Thus far we have written solely about worker directors. This is primarily because the Bullock Report recommended this system. However, the terms of reference of the committee precluded discussion of other methods and these must be discussed in the context of the present debate.

Many trade unionists, both white-collar and manual workers dislike the concept of worker directors. There are three basic reasons: the first is a fear of the responsibilities involved; the second is a fear that the traditional union bargaining mechanisms would be pre-empted and/or compromised (this latter argument is the more widespread and there must be some truth in it). Clearly joint decisions will carry much more weight and the job of the union official arguing against decisions made by union members on the board is not to be envied. This is the reaction versus pre-emption argument.

However, this latter argument leads us on to the third opposition position: worker directors are not, and will not, be representative of all the workers – again there has to be some truth in this. Worker directors will have to be men and women of exceptional ability and character as in some cases it would mean that industrial democracy would be served by ten trade unionists representing 100,000 workers.

Plant, divisional and group union/management democracy committees are not out of the question. Indeed they fit hand-in-glove with worker directors and with planning agreements and these together could form the basis for genuine industrial democracy embracing all employees. Indeed, they form probably the only practicable basis.

One set of opponents of worker directors are those who believe that the only real industrial democracy must come through an extension of collective bargaining. Although this is a genuinely held belief and one which has more than a superficial attraction, it has not been coherently thought through and we feel that some time should be spent in discussing it.

First, it is no more democratic in a devolvement sense than the worker-director plan. As large employers are involved and these are all multi-plant at the least, any extension of collective bargaining would have to be at a group or national level and this, in turn, involves few people. Second, it is almost inconceivable to write a procedure agreement which would be capable of delineating both the topics that could be bargained and the procedure for doing so. Is it seriously suggested that before each yearly stage of a rolling corporate plan unions sit down and negotiate its details? That would not only be unworkable and inefficient, it would also set union member against union member, plant against plant and division against division. Is it seriously suggested that if company 'X' refuses to invest £10 million in, say, Humberside, the unions will take sanctions against the company? If it is not, then we do not have bargaining; we are back to consultations. These are the semblances of power without the power, but with all the responsibilities – to turn Baldwin's *bon mot* on its head, this is the prerogative of the solicited.

The proponents of the extension of collective bargaining always point to Fiat in Italy as the ideal. It is true that they have an agreement – it is untrue that it has achieved anything worthwhile. Yet the concept is still correct, but as with so much of industrial relations it is the mechanism that must be refined. Worker directors could be seen as extending collective bargaining into the boardroom. If the joint union committees represented through all levels of enterprise have equal inputs for decisions made at the appropriate levels and planning agreements cement these relationships with government, too, then the horizons will be well and truly widened.

Even so, there are logistical difficulties. The problem as we see it is not to do with company size, although this is important, but the diversity of different types. In particular, there are four types of company which present special difficulties: the foreign-owned multinational; the British-owned, multi-company conglomerate; the holding company, and the private, family company.

Clearly, the problems are inter-related, especially so far as the first three categories are concerned, but the problem with the foreign-owned multinational, is that directors and managers of UK subsidiaries have, at the moment, only limited control. The introduction of worker directors and the other elements will certainly not change that, although there may be leverage in an EEC context. Any legislation of course can (and should) be extended to foreign-owned companies registered in the UK, but there will still be a situation where worker directors have access to only partially effective levels of power.

In many instances, the multi-company conglomerate suffers the same kind of problem as those described above, but there are some special problems, even where the parent company is British-owned. Many of the largest of these types of company (Courtaulds, ICI, Commercial Union, and so on) have extremely complex, interlocking patterns of ownership. Each separately registered company within a group will have its own directors, but they very often do not function as effective boards in the usual way. Ideally, of course, there should be provision for worker directors at each level of board, as well as on the parent board. Many of the companies in the empires of Courtaulds or Unilevers are very small, however, and might be excluded from legislation if there is a cut-off point based on number of employees. Setting that aside, however, there is still the problem of establishing a mechanism for electing representatives to the parent board and on inter-union committees. The ICI entry in *Who Owns Whom* for example, includes more than 100 companies in the UK alone; in the case of Courtaulds, there are more than 400.

A variant of this type of problem concerns the holding company, which may administer the affairs of many subsidiaries but which is itself non-productive. Such companies may very well be excluded if company size is judged simply by employees, as holding companies do not normally have any, beyond a small secretariat. Just as with multinationals, the effectiveness of worker directors would be limited if representation were restricted to subsidiary boards without involvement at the level where many of the important decisions are taken. In all of these instances the importance of the lower echelons of industrial democratic procedures and of planning agreements is paramount.

Finally, there is the private, family company. In Germany these companies are excluded from the obligation to have employee representatives on the board, even when there are more than 500 employees. There is no reason, in principle, why private companies should be excluded; all are obliged to have directors, so there seems no reason why their boards should not include employee representatives.

In common to all these types of companies is that the white-collar workforce is basically interchangeable, and one union group in an enterprise easily recognises and emulates gains made by a comparable group elsewhere: this is bound to accelerate participation once it becomes established in the UK. The huge new task will be that of training union representatives. The Swedish unions have access to an additional £10 million annually to help with joint decision-taking training and this is in addition to the existing heavy funding of union education. If this amount of money per worker was translated into the British equivalent, it would amount to a yearly grant of at least £80 million.

Information, as we have mentioned, is of crucial importance. From a trade union point of view it could be counter-productive to have members on the board or on plant or divisional joint union teams who could not either fully understand the documentation, or be in a position to have it analysed for them. It has been shown that what is needed is not the sophisticated argument, but the good trade unionist taking his or her stand. This is a superficially attractive notion. What is going to happen when a good trade unionist argues strongly against future redundancies at a board meeting having just approved a document which he did not fully understand and which, in investment terms, made those redundancies inevitable? This will happen time and time again unless the unions educate their own membership in general and their worker directors in particular. The white-collar employee, with his technical or managerial skills can be of great assistance on the board, provided he has a right to be there. Some people consider that management should not be represented on the board, nor should it be allowed to vote, but this confusion of manager and owner is about as misguided as the confusion between wealth and income. Provided that the inevitable teething problems can be overcome, there is every reason to hope for great things from industrial democracy. It will widen collective bargaining and add to the unions' role in planning and decision-making rather than in simply reacting. The public sector has different problems: the nationalised industries should be the easiest of all to deal with, but the civil service and local government are the most difficult, for here the problem is that of dealing with an elected employer. Although some system may be worked out, it is unlikely to be very meaningful. As the chairman of a London borough put it: if the trade unions want seats on the council or council committees the electors of the borough could, and will in the equity due to the democratic process, demand seats on that union's executive.

Paradoxically, all these moves give the greater challenge to white-collar unions. In the entire trade union movement, the unions are the ones nearest to the power centres in terms of membership, yet it is precisely because the members are so near, yet in practice so far, from important decision-making that gives the challenge. These unions, in both the private and public sectors have members equipped and trained to make serious logistical contributions to managements. They have been critical of existing policies within their industries, their companies and their sectors, not from a politically motivated standpoint, but from a position of in-depth knowledge. This enables them to see injustices, misallocation of resources and sheer incompetence from a practical view and to propose sensible, if sometimes radical, changes.

The challenge, however, is tinged with misgiving. Few managers worth their salt want their judgment challenged or decision changed by people who they consider unqualified to criticise – whether or not those managers are union members. Most managers still subscribe, if only notionally, to the concept of individual discretion and abhor decisions by committee, despite the fact that the overwhelming majority have little or no personal initiative allowed to them and their decisions are already circumscribed by committee decisions.

Union members have a lot to offer in terms of both original thought and practical common sense and the managers would be well advised to harness this untapped and often despised source. Second, managers should be able to increase their personal initiatives under a democratic system providing they join it – not watch it from the outside. Certainly there will be fears – all changes and uncertainties create these, but they are unjustified. A rearguard action by managers to protect what they see as encroachment on their preserves, against the tide of Western European history, would be as unwelcome as it would be unwise.

The final, widening horizon is one which again is being discussed but at present has not yet been the subject of legislation. This is worker-trustees or members of pension fund boards or committees of management. This is a complicated and far reaching subject which, with all its ramifications and implications, could justify a book on its own. As many of these involve national economies and industrial strategies, we shall be brief and only sketch in the background.

Throughout this book we have mentioned pension funds. For a white-collar union, pensions are of considerable importance. This is probably because of the type of member in these unions and their typical middle-class preoccupation with security. It has always seemed illogical to the unions that the trustees of pension funds have invariably been appointed by management on an oligarchical basis when these funds were held in trust for all the employees. The government issued a White Paper on the subject in 1976 and legislation to provide for a 50 per cent membership on boards made up of independent recognised union members has been promised. This proposal, probably even more than the Bullock Report, produced the most hostile reactions from the CBI and other employers' bodies. Why? If all the monies are wisely invested and distributed, there is nothing to hide and union nominees will have a sinecure. We are led to believe this is the case, though we doubt this; indeed, we know this is not true. Pension-fund monies have been used to buy shares in the employer's own company to ward off take-overs; have been used to buy the company's properties which are then leased back at nominal rents; have been used to provide cheap and long mortgages for the favoured few and have been used to provide commission splitting for the brokers and accepting houses concerned. No wonder employees are worried – all trust deeds are supposed to bind trustees to make the members' interest paramount. Monies have also been used to buy property, at home and abroad, and works of art rather than investing in productive industry; but this takes us into a different realm of argument. Suffice to say we believe that the members' interests are better served by taking a long-term rather than the short-term view which prevails today.

The opposition is now centred upon the concept of unions rather than member participation. Unions are the only logical method by which proper representation can be assured. The majority of pension funds (in number) are those catering for white-collar employees. Certainly there are non-union members in big schemes, but they are all perfectly capable of joining a union if they feel disenfranchised. If, however, they feel they are management and thus cannot join a union, then they can avail themselves of the 50 per cent of management seats on the board – that, surely, is logical. Union member trustees are not only a long-overdue step forward. They will enable employees to control the return and distribution of both their own contributions and the deferred salary paid by their employer. Yet again to do so there will have to be a rapid education programme, which will have to concentrate on investment analysis, on trustee law and on pension fund law.

White-collar workers are all involved in this change. In most enterprises unions will find members who revel in the most complex of pension fund calculations and the most abstruse and sometimes inventive interpretations of the law. These people have an immense amount to offer. In addition at least one union, ASTMS, has pension-fund experts and actuaries in membership and their expertise, although being tapped, is still not fully realised.

The total amounts of money involved are frighteningly large. Pension funds are now the largest, single institutional investor, having overtaken the insurance companies in 1977. Both the private-sector and the huge public-sector funds wield a potential power which, at present, is mainly unaccountable. This cannot be good for other members of the fund, or indeed for the economy in general. This wider point is one which the committee chaired by Sir Harold Wilson is now looking at closely.

At the end of the day, there will be a better and more fulfilled labour force, managerial, white-collar skilled and unskilled. It is a logical extension of current trends; it is a step towards recognising that self-determination does not stop at the ballot box, but should embrace the totality of life.

Chapter 10

The impact of the white-collar union on Britain

'Change is not made without inconvenience, even from worse to better.' – Hooker

As the middle class, for the first time, is poised to move into positions of administrative power as of right what effect, if any, has the white-collar union movement had on the social stratification in Britain so far? Britain is a status-conscious, class-ridden society where education and accent plays a large part in the social standing of an individual, where shop-floor workers are not only separated in the work environment from the management but are separated in attitudes and culture. Some proponents of white-collar unions have strenuously defended the idea that there is a move towards the proletarianisation of the salariat – assuming that the act of joining a union had the immediate effect of making an individual shrug off the attitudes acquired throughout life and sustained by the media. Others will stick to the embourgeoisement thesis that as the manual workers get higher real wages and higher standards of living, they will somehow become middle-class. Neither of these theories would appear to be borne out by the known developments.

The middle classes join trade unions because they need to. At first it does not seem to matter to them whether they want to or not. They have to because they realise that they need protection, and they need expertise. Many of them appreciate the contradiction in applying to join a trade union because they have always believed in individual initiative as opposed to group action. Nevertheless, economic circumstances have dictated that the individual is increasingly vulnerable in collective bargaining situations and can only counterbalance this by combining with colleagues. It is true, however, that joining a trade union is an act which specifically acknowledges the fact that despite skills, status experience and education, employees are employees. This does not however argue a new identification with manual workers or even other members of the same union. This comes sometimes swiftly, sometimes slowly, but it is not even certain that it will always come.

These statements are, of course, generalisations. To see whether they are borne out and to what extent, one has to look at some of the categories of employees who join white-collar unions. Foremen and supervisors generally get promoted from the shop floor and would now be expected to make the transition without any problems. But there used to be the most rigid separation at the time of promotion when the new staff member would resign his union membership and, indeed, his manual union would not wish him to retain it. The next group are the technical employees. Some have degrees or diplomas from qualifying bodies. Unionisation has little social consequence in the main because the background of this group, except for some engineers in professional institutions, tends to provide an acceptance of trade unions. Clerical, administrative and managerial staff are somewhat different. For the career personnel there used to be a central dilemma because their background is either non-union or so lightly organised that the unions have seemed alien and an uncertain substitute for the stable and permanent employer of the past. This does not hold good for public employment where union membership has been encouraged since 1919. In the medium term, at least, it is significant that so many previously non-unionised people have opted to join TUC-affiliates rather than the quasi-unions or staff associations.

It seems that once the decision is taken it is taken wholeheartedly. Unions have an important educational function not only in the collective-bargaining world but also in the wider sense. Many people are now having for the first time an exposure to trade union methods, mechanisms, officials and policies. The middle-class fear of unions starts to diminish as the exposure continues and although there may be disagreement on policies and tactics there is nevertheless an acceptance of both the right of the union to adopt them and some understanding of the reasons why they did so. This is the most significant aspect.

Politically, at least three million trade unionists must vote Conservative, although that does not necessarily make them party workers or subscribers. Obviously a proportion of these will be in white-collar unions. One surprise of white-collar unionism is in the political stances adopted by the unions concerned: ASTMS has always been a progressive union with policies based most firmly on free collective bargaining. TASS has similarly been on the progressive, or in party political terms, left wing of the movement. In the Civil Service the CPSA and the SCS have favoured non-establishment policies and these are the unlikeliest of unions to adopt such postures. Yet, oddly the policy battles are not between right and left but between left-of-centre and ultra-left. The social stratification impact of white-collar unions has probably been slight in the short-term and so has the political impact – in spite of the leftist political phenomena. It is very much as though members actively divorce the industrial objectives and their own personal objectives from the political function of the union and that providing the union continues to act successfully on their behalf this is all that is required. The level of contracting out of the political levy would tend to reinforce this view.

The growth of white-collar trade unionism has taken many people by surprise and not least the larger, more traditional trade unions themselves: NALGO is the fifth largest union, ASTMS the sixth, NUT the eleventh and CPSA the twelfth in the TUC (not including NUPE and USDAW at fourth and eighth, both with substantial white-collar membership). We have looked at the changes in General Council representation that have occurred but not at attitudes. The TUC is still manual-worker orientated but since manual workers are still the majority and considering that the growth of white-collar representation is so recent, this is not surprising. This attitude has historically caused some difficulties where the TUC represents the view of all unions, for example, problems which arise over occupational pension schemes and incremental payments.

But attitudes are changing very rapidly, though difficulties do arise, and it would be incomplete not to record them. The £6 policy, for example, had a cut-off point of £8,500 per annum and people earning more than this could not get either incremental or principal increases. Some TUC leaders wanted it pitched at £7,000. But ASTMS, the SCS, and NALGO would have then been precluded from negotiating for a substantial minority of their members even at the higher figure. The 5-per-cent policy perpetuated the problem, but this is not all. White-collar unions often have very different problems and preoccupations to those of other trade unions. Considerations, such as the incidence of taxation, can engender considerable differences: attitudes to overtime and incremental scales also provoke discussion. In addition, there are a host of individual union problems ranging from problems with a staff association and Certification Officer difficulties, to the difficulty of measuring productivity in a drawing office which is not within the experience of other TUC affiliates.

The growth of white-collar union membership has however had a profound effect on industrial relations at plant level and on the TUC itself. At plant level, the fact that staff (especially supervisory and line management) will not do manual workers' jobs during a dispute has aided those unions and their members considerably. The widespread nature of the growth now means that nearly all manual unions have been affected. At a national level the ingenuity that white-collar unions have had to pursue has had its effect on the TUC. That body now prepares more detailed and more sophisticated briefs and reports as failure to do so invites an invidious comparison with certain head-offices' activities. At the same time, white-collar unions have their way more in the TUC industry committees, on the sector working parties and into NEDCs. They have brought with them the back up from research and legal departments and have thus stimulated the challenging and questioning of facts and arguments presented by governments' employees which were previously quietly accepted.

Employers, as we have noted, still react strongly against white-collar unions and still attempt to forestall recognition for as long as possible. In the last few years, however, a growing group of them have come to accept the fact of organisation if only because they bring order and stability to their industrial relations policies. But the resentment is still there in certain companies especially for the managerial grades (as we shall see in the next chapter).

When Ray Gunter called the Ministry of Labour 'my bed of nails', he was mainly concerned with manual workers. Successive ministers have progressively realised that white-collar unions have to be catered for too. We have outlined their growing militancy earlier in the book and certainly Ray Gunter would not have dreamed of disputes by civil servants or electrical power engineers, let alone doctors or computer personnel.

In a working sense too the white-collar unions have had an impact. They tend to use government departments, lobby and buttonhole Ministers more than ever before. It makes those who rule realise that there is a growing awareness and alertness to problems and this is not confined to the miners or car workers. It is now unthinkable that there could ever be a mass intervention from volunteers from the middle classes in a national dispute. The truth is that many white-collar workers in both sectors have begun to despise their lives of genteel poverty and have discovered that the world has more to offer them. In doing this they also have had to discover the bargaining power latent in their collective strength and it is this realisation which will probably have the longest lasting and most radical effect.

The white-collar union is just starting to make its mark on society. It is new, it is learning and it is growing. Society created it and in turn it is starting to have a hand in shaping society and its appetites for advance stimulate change.

Chapter 11

Managers   _See_ Anthony) C 14, also C 12.
I of W:)

'Who can control his fate?' – Othello

There is no such thing as 'a manager'. It is a collective noun like 'professional' which embraces a range from the carriage of arms to the plying of the oldest trade. Indeed, it goes even further than this. Most people can recognise a soldier or a whore: the same can hardly be held true for managers. One man's manager is another's messenger or oppressor. The style and status are all rooted in their personal data and prejudices the eye of the beholder.

All available writings and arithmetic would tend to reinforce this view. Different salary surveys give a remarkably large range of salaries, fringe benefits and job descriptions for single job titles. Even definitions of the broad category areas such as lower, middle and higher or upper management vary widely, even though the responsibilities and duties, perquisites and bonuses, and more recently the status of managers are now in the area of public consciousness and debate. A vigorous tax concessions lobby has concentrated on managers and the disincentive effects of high marginal rates of tax, whilst some spokesmen of the British Institute of Management and the Institute of Directors have rushed to their defence in the face of real or imagined attacks. All this has brought the manager more sharply into focus and in the forefront of political public life than ever before.

The 1971 Census identified just over 1·6 million managers and of these 1·35 million were men and 262,000 were women. They are, thus, in substantial numbers comprising roughly 6 per cent of the workforce.

It might be as well, at this point, to define what *we* mean by 'managers'. They are those employees who take decisions and then accept the responsibility for these decisions on behalf of an enterprise, a department of an enterprise, or a department itself. This is further refined by defining a starting point as <u>one above</u> the senior supervisor. This is not to say that supervisors do not have management functions; they do, but nevertheless they are not in our definition.

140

Chapter 12

The quality of life

'Increased means and increased leisure are the two civilizers of man.' –
Disraeli

Playwrights and novelists down the ages have observed, with varying
degrees of elegance, that man's allotted span is both finite and brief.
Within this lifetime the overwhelming majority of people have to work
and the amount of time spent actually at the workplace is large. The
average white-collar worker, leaving school at eighteen and working to
sixty-five on a mere 38-hour week will spend over nine years of his life
at work. This does not include overtime; it does not include taking
work home; it does not include travelling to and from work. A more
realistic figure is probably nearer to eleven years.

Work has been dignified, sanctified, praised and elevated to the status
of religion, but almost always by those whose necessity to work has
been limited. Indeed, why do we work? Why have we elevated it to its
present status. Is it indeed a good thing? Can modern industrial society
sustain work for all and should trade unions continue to press for it to
do so? What fundamental changes should be made in work patterns and
the working lifetime? These are the questions that we intend to pose in
this chapter. Hopefully we shall attempt to answer them although many
readers will disagree with both our analyses and the methods of resolution which we suggest. This however is all to the good. Work, leisure
and the quality of life is a subject which not only requires more attention but the time-scale in which discussions can take place before events
overtake us is getting shorter – there is a degree of urgency. If this short
contribution goes some way to stimulating the debate then it will have
served a more than useful purpose.

The preoccupation with work is a relic from the pre-industrial
revolution and then the labour-intensive days. In an agriculturally based
society where consumer goods were crafted in cottage industries, work
had a real meaning – it was survival. Food and clothing and a dwelling
place were essential. Each inactive member of the family unit was,
basically, a drain on the work unit – it was an inescapable fact of life.

151

But not everyone worked, as John Bull so wryly noted. As the cities grew, as agriculture became more efficient and the trade-craft and merchant classes grew, so the emphasis on work changed. No longer could the family unit support itself by working on the land; people had to work for money to buy goods and clothes.

It was clearly always in someone's interests to have others work harder. The church through tithes, the lord of the manor through tributes and taxes, the journeyman through more apprentices to give the guild master more returns and therefore more leisure. To industrialise there needs to be a surplus which is ploughed back into investment. This can come from profits or savings or both. The industrial revolution was firmly based on profits, the fruits of others working hard and on the savings of a few. The Protestant ethic, which gripped Britain so hard at the time, not only postulated that hard work was good and the harder the better, but that savings were good too. It is clear however that the majority worked and the minority saved, making it a very bifurcated ethic.

Work was praised from the pulpit, in parliament, by social reformers (the workhouse was supposed to be an advanced form of charity) and by employers. Poems were written eulogising it, of the noble sweat-of-the-brow variety, and writings elevated it. The rudimentary trade unions however had other views. They were meeting and organising on the premise that there was too much of it and that, furthermore, its intrinsic value was far less than the compensatory wages. Waiting for a good return in the kingdom of heaven they argued was not sufficient to justify family poverty, malnutrition and, in truth, an early visit to paradise.

At the time when British productivity, inventiveness and output were at their peak, the quality of life of the British people was near to its nadir. Of course apprentices brought from the workhouses who had to sleep under their machines and the women working in coal mines were thought by some to be undergoing elevating experiences. Equally, the housing of workers was bad, social services non-existent, education rudimentary, health care superstition-bound and civil liberties backward. In essence, there were several generations of workers sacrificed to profit and through profit, the industrial revolution, both in Britain and in the Empire was not the golden age that has been portrayed.

The work ethic became ingrained during this period. The recurrent bouts of depression and unemployment have always been opposed by trade unions and employees on two distinct grounds. The obvious one is the lack of money that unemployment brings with it. Clearly at times when there was no unemployment pay and no social service provision this had a more serious impact. The second reason however is that by depriving a man or woman of work, a loss of dignity or even identity is involved and this reason owed much to the religious interpretation and teachings of the time. This attitude still prevails today for somewhat different reasons imposed by the current moralities.

Unemployment is still regarded as a curse and those unemployed often feel pariahs, especially in white-collar and managerial circles. Society still demands a respect for work and those working and still regards those not working as somehow responsible for their own 'unfortunate position', rather like the Victorian attitude to 'fallen women'. Society, as we have suggested earlier, is built around rising expectations. To cut people off from this basic drive is to inflict considerable damage. Despite the fact we now have unemployment benefits and supplementary benefits the reductions in real income are often severe, especially in the managerial areas. There has been much media comment on scroungers and idlers, yet earnings-related benefit is both low and short-lived and the dole-queue-benefit-application system humilating. Few people choose to be unemployed if there are reasonable alternatives.

The impact of unemployment on the young is severe too. Our education system is geared to learning for work, yet we find many school-leavers unable to put their schooling into practice. Those affected see this as a betrayal by their seniors. More education is certainly not a long-term answer, although different education is another matter. So from the young upwards the work ethic is ingrained in the British consciousness although, as we shall argue, this is changing in some respects.

The notion of work thus provokes an ambivalent response. It is both desirable and unpleasant, both a necessity and a chore. For most people in Britain it is unpleasant in some degree; few employees will readily admit to enjoying their jobs and those who do tend to be in professions, in creative employments or in decision-making positions. This is not however an attitude confined to Britain. An old Haitian proverb states: 'If work were a good thing, the rich would have found a way of keeping it all to themselves.' In economic jargon terms work is a disutility and payment is the compensating factor.

The depressing feature of this is that as technology changes and improves so the dislike and boredom increases, or so the literature on the subject would tend to suggest. Crafts and skills have given way to machines and automation; production-line techniques breed repetitive jobs and the larger units in government, commerce and industry have created the white-collar 'line'. Specialisation is often efficient, but it is not necessarily the most enjoyable way of spending one's working life, especially if it is both narrowly defined and immutable. There are signs in Britain that technologically based industries and systems are poised to 'take-off'. These are not necessarily of the moving-production-line principle, but may well entail the adaptation of advanced technologies to do jobs for which they were not originally designed. Lasers are now being used in many industrial processes and the spread into others, now that the portable, movable and focusable machines have been developed, cannot be long delayed. Micro-computers giving the same power as the large, main frame installations for at less than ½ per cent of the cost are a reality in the UK and moving to Europe. The petrochemical industry, so vital to the medium term prospects of Britain, is highly capital intensive.

In short, most of the advances which have been, or will be made in the industrial, commercial and even government sectors of the economy will require fewer people to operate in these sectors. Thus each marginal investment will require fewer employees and if this investment replaces an existing method, jobs will actually be lost overall. The alternative is to keep the same manning levels, thus reducing productivity on the grounds that this is socially desirable, and indeed less expensive, than paying unemployment pay and all the ancillary benefits. This has been the argument in many private- and public-sector enterprises. It does, however, lean heavily on the argument that *work*, in itself, *is a good thing*. Given North Sea Oil revenues and relief on the balance of payments, the underlying conditions are present for an investment boom and, most importantly, a boom based on efficiency and productivity rather than on vastly increased demand for goods and services.

These factors, along with an expected increase in the labour force in excess of one million over the next decade, and with the high probability of sluggish world trade, argues that there will be a real increase in unemployment on a structural basis for some time to come. For a country with an ingrained work ethic this poses serious problems and for a society which relies on the growth of expectations, these problems are multiplied. The Sudreau Report characterised this trend quite trenchantly. It suggested that as educational and technological advances proceed, we are producing more highly educated young people for whom there are fewer jobs in total and fewer jobs where they can make use of their increased qualifications. This is a recipe for disaster. We can already see school-leavers and graduate unemployment rising and doing so with each successive slump. There is a high degree of boredom, juvenile delinquency and street violence and although one cannot positively say they are as a result of employment conditions and prospects, it would be foolhardy to deny a relationship.

This gives us different but inter-related problems. Decreasing opportunities to work combined with dissatisfaction with work is virtually impossible to measure, and manifests itself in many ways. Some employees may want responsibility, others are literally made ill by it; some prefer repetitive jobs whilst others find them soul-destroying. The

Department of Employment Work Unit states:

> The few skills required, the repetitiveness of so many jobs, the lack of freedom to make decisions, the impersonal nature of organisations and the relentlessness of paced work. The result is that jobs are often felt to be monotonous, trivial, meaningless, restricting and sometimes impose too great a stress.

It has been assumed that these factors apply exclusively to the manual workers, but as we have seen in an earlier chapter, they apply to white-collar and managerial workers in equal measure.

The vital and fundamental question which arises from this is do we live to work or do we work to live? Looked at in this context, policies which reduce the dole queues but replace this evil with other evils are not a step forward and may even be counter-productive. This would arise if job creation was to be based on the assumption that all jobs are equal and if the answer to the above question is that we live to work. Surely the trade union movement should have as its slogan 'The Right to Leisure'. We shall look at this from two standpoints: that of the present and that of the future.

Our thesis is based on the view of the director-general of the International Labour Office: 'the promotion of a better balance between the working life and personal life for each and every person'. This will inevitably mean finding acceptable substitutes (remunerated or subsidised) for work such as more education, recycling and updating of skills, leisure activities and a restructuring of the working life. Although this sounds an imposing list of demands it is one that will be increasingly made. We can see in some industries and sectors of the economy an unofficial three-day weekend. Employees are voting with their feet and voluntarily receiving less money whilst opting for increased leisure. There is no marginal tax argument here, the majority of these employees pay standard-rate tax on all earnings; it is less a lack of incentives than a positive dislike of work. This is, in the long run, a healthy reaction. It is the first stage in the disintegration of the national work ethic. Could it be that British employees, the first to take part in the industrial revolution, have decided that enough is enough and will be the first to stimulate the 'leisure revolution'?

At present there is a real unemployment rate of over two million, if those not registering (mainly married women) are included. Paradoxically there is a considerable amount of overtime being worked. Those who do work often have to conform to shift systems – this is not only true of the production-line worker, but also includes continuous-process operations, both manufacturing and computer, nurses, doctors, police, firemen and a host of other public-utility employees. Quite often these shifts include working anti-social hours, and the life of the employee suffers correspondingly.

Early studies in 1921 and then in 1938 suggested that shift workers suffered an abnormally high incidence of stomach disorder and, indeed, showed that stomach ulcers were eight times more likely than for employees working in accord with natural rhythms. Although recent studies have not confirmed these findings the suggestion is that shift working has now become voluntary and thus the stresses have declined. However other stress-related diseases such as coronary thrombosis, psoriasis, etc., do appear to have a positive correlation with shift work patterns.

We have previously discussed stress at work and the difficulties in both isolating it and dealing with it. There is however an associated stress and that is travel to work. One of the less researched facets of work is the compulsion of attendance. In conversations around the country the sentiment is expressed that one of the worst parts of work is having to get out of bed in the morning and the travel afterwards; this is especially true for those working in big cities. The average journey for an employee working in Central London is fifty minutes. Although London Allowance is partially designed to cope with this extra disutility it cannot do so in its entirety. Whether an employee is travelling by public or private transport, the conditions of travelling are uncongenial and frustrating. The rush hours, both to and from work, are one of the least desirable developments of the twentieth century. They do not apply only to London, even the smaller provincial cities such as Exeter have developed them and wherever they are they add to the personal cost of going to work.

These are, however, all comparatively minor questions when compared with the more fundamental choices available on working life times. The major leisure times available to employees in life are pre-work holidays from school, or at higher educational establishments, or after retirement age. The rest of life in between, in fact the majority of life, is devoted to work, with short recuperative breaks each year. We must ask, is this the ideal situation and if not, are there any practicable policies that can be embraced which will change this situation? If people believe that 'we live to work' this approach would have little to commend it; however, the authors believe that although the work ethic is deeply ingrained it is not incompatible with changes in work patterns. The increasing pressure of claims for increased holiday entitlements and shorter working weeks would tend to support this view.

It does seem incomprehensible that extensive leisure times are available when people are the least equipped to use them; they have either not learned to do so, or are physically not capable of doing so. It is equally strange that leisure is generally most restricted at the time when it is most needed, when children are growing and family life is most important: there must be hundreds of thousands of children who rarely see their fathers. In all logic it does seem incomprehensible that rest and leisure is allowed, in large measure, only after retirement. Reputable medical and psychological research suggests that people's efficiency falls dramatically after continuous periods of work and that this is especially so in jobs requiring skill, judgment or imagination. It would seem to everyone's interests, both employers and employees, to revise attitudes on leisure.

We believe that there are two reinforcing imperatives to change the work patterns of Britain towards favouring the quality of life. The first is that existing practices need overhauling. The second is that future patterns of production and the known and potential technological changes will make this essential. We have written about the political and economic changes which will also have to take place to accommodate these changes in the book *Computers and the Unions* and we believe that the two must proceed simultaneously.

There are many things that can and should be done. Two of them are under discussion at present, so we shall deal with these first: the 35-hour week and early retirement. The 1977 TUC Congress passed a composite resolution favouring the 35-hour week and, in addition, to one which set up a committee to examine the quality of working life. There is also an Anglo-German trade union initiative on the subject. As with so many things it does sound attractive on a superficial level, but on examination disadvantages become apparent. One argument regularly used against the shorter working week is that it would be commercial and economic suicide. This has been deployed down the ages in attempts to stop social reforms: the abolition of slavery in the USA, the stopping of children working, universal education, the removal of health hazards in a multitude of processes and the wage demands in the 1930s. Subsequent events proved that the prophesied Nemesis did not materialise. It would be the same with the 35-hour week.

One most interesting fact is that when, in 1974, the nation was put onto the three-day week as a result of the miners' dispute, the index of industrial production fell by only 5½ per cent yet hours worked were 40 per cent lower. Even allowing for inaccuracies in the statistics, it is clear that productivity must have risen considerably. Using a slightly different measure, the index of production has (with hiccoughs) continued to rise over the last thirty years, whilst hours of work have decreased. It could well be argued that a cut in basic hours will actually stimulate performance and productivity and that even if overtime is banned and more people employed, the increased revenue created will outweigh the increased payroll costs. This would of course vary on a company, industry or sectoral basis, as well as on technical and process bases. The rationale behind it is simple. Employees cannot sustain optimal performance levels throughout a day or week and the longer the day or week the greater the percentage level of sub-optimal performance. This is, however, only the negative side of the question. The positive side is that it is probable that the relationship between hours of work and efficiency is not a linear one, that is, it does not run proportionately on a 1:1 or 2:1 basis. It is more likely to be on the basis of the more hours of work the greater the percentage of sub-optimal performance. Whether this is due to boredom, stress, tiredness, or whatever, it has been found to be true of airline pilots, managers, doctors, and in several academically oriented practical experiments. The underlying proposition is quite simple, 'all work and no play make Jack and Jill dull people'.

The 35-hour week does however pose other problems. In continuous-process operations and on other round-the-clock operations the shift patterns created would, if anything, decrease the quality of life. For many managers and doctors the scheme would be impracticable. Also it would not solve the problem of working days. A 35-hour week, spread over five days, is already common in clerical working areas, especially in London and it means that the struggle of getting to and from work and the preparations for doing so, probably the most disagreeable part of the work process, is unchanged. We shall argue that a wider and more flexible approach should be taken.

Earlier retirement has been a constant aim of the trade union movement, reinforced by TUC Congress decisions in 1976 which proposed a common (male-female) retirement age of sixty, but again this may not be the most favourable policy for employees in general. The early deaths of men and women who retire early does not suggest that the policy is altogether a good thing, although cynically, one can argue that it does favour pension funds. The present level of pensions would mean more people living in greater poverty, or near poverty, if people lived as long as before or, alternatively, a vast amount of money transferred into the pensions sector. Too many employees have been made dependent upon work; it has become the reason for living and cutting this off prematurely can have disastrous effects. Socially too the effect can be great in that many employees have their social life revolving around work and their workmates, and this contact suddenly ceases. There can be no doubt that the feeling in some industries is overwhelmingly in favour of earlier retirement – the mining industry, for example. However, the miners are one of the few groups of workers who live in close mutually self-reinforcing groups and many of the social problems on retirement thus disappear.

There are many other ideas which could profitably be explored; some of them have already received mention in Chapter 7, but need far wider application. Flexitime, money and material compensations, good sick-pay schemes, health and safety committees, voluntary and early retirement schemes, longer holidays; all have a part to play, as indeed does industrial democracy. There are, however, other matters.

The working day, week, month, or year does need to be looked at. If the known technologies expand in the way that has been predicted and new technologies follow in their wake, there will be fewer jobs available. The traditional answer to this is to expand the service sector, especially the government service sector, in order to 'mop-up' the unemployment. Aside from the retraining aspects and the labour mobility problems such a solution implies, it is clear that the service sector itself is becoming more capital intensive and technology will impact there as much as in other sectors. If this is the case we shall be reaching a situation where 'licences to work' will have to be issued.

Let us take this situation a little further. If the investment and consequent changes are forthcoming it also argues that industry and commerce are more efficient and creating a greater surplus. This must not be confused with return on capital because as technological change brings both shorter equipment life and higher costs, so returns on capital will fall, over the long run. This surplus will have to be used, in part, to pay for those unemployed and to pay for those employed for shorter periods. The alternative to this is to run an economy which has an increasingly inequitable distribution of wealth and income and an increasing concentration of economic power and leverage. As with permanent incomes policies such a situation would probably need a dictatorship to maintain it.

If there is to be an element of work-sharing we believe it should be based on the number of days worked. In 1972 the TUC stated that 'attention should also be given to securing the four-day working week'. This simple concept appears to have fallen by the wayside, but has a lot to commend it. Most people, if given the choice, would prefer to work a 35-hour week over four days rather than five; certainly, when such a choice has been given the entire day off has been preferred: the problems of getting up, of preparation and of travel obviously weigh heavily. The four-day week also avoids many of the shift pattern problems and thus, decreased quality of lives. In some industries it might be appropriate, in others not, we will have to be flexible. The same applies to systems where there are three weeks on and one week off, or three months on and one month off. Systems such as these are not impossible. The North Sea oil rigs use them and many employers in the Middle East use them.

Early retirement is the other solution we referred to. We prefer a system which is flexible. The retirement ages of men and women should be standardised and we believe these should be discretionary at any time between the ages of sixty and sixty-five. We do not exclude voluntary early retirement before this – from age fifty upwards, although we do believe that more, and better, information should be given to employees interested in this proposition. Too often employees have been dazzled by the prospect of a lump-sum payment, often the largest they have ever held and retired into delayed poverty. On the other side of the coin we do tend to lose employees of considerable ability, experience and wisdom, by having arbitrary retirement ages. There must be provision for tapping these talents, if the people concerned agree, to the benefit of all concerned. This could be done in one of the more certain growth industries – leisure – and nowhere is such use more needed than in pre-retirement, educational and leisure courses themselves.

Other changes which should be made include sabbatical leave, well known and used in academic circles; we believe that everyone would benefit from such prolonged study periods. The study need not be academic at all, it could entail the widening of personal experiences and there should be provision for at least two of these leaves in a working lifetime. Other possible changes, such as paternity leave on the Swedish or French lines and job-swapping in appropriate circumstances, should be encouraged.

One thing all this will mean is education, or so it seems. The argument that employees who suddenly have leisure time will only waste it doing trivial things, or rapidly become bored, is an extension of our underlying work ethos. No one has tested it since those with the most leisure (of working age) are those unemployed and the majority of these are involuntarily so. There is an implicit arrogance in the suggestion and those who make it most regularly are generally those with a considerable educational background imposing their own value judgments on those who have not attained their exalted level. Nevertheless, there is probably some case that can be made and also one must consider that the employees themselves will demand increased education facilities. These fall into two distinct categories: vocational and pleasurable.

The first must be treated more seriously than hitherto. It is just not good enough to provide courses in welding or bricklaying and other trades; these have a part to play but are not the totality. We must look at more fundamental changes in our educational system, changes which ultimately would lead to life-long education. Why should early omissions or decisions determine the pattern of a person's life? Languages, sciences and fundamental disciplines can be taught far more readily to mature people who know what they want to do. Our system traps us into inescapable culs-de-sac at an unacceptably early age and we must be prepared to amend it. Running alongside this is the ineluctable fact that skills are becoming obsolescent as each year passes and this is especially true in the scientifically and technically based employments.

Unions, especially the white-collar ones, must ensure that the employees in these jobs have the educational opportunities to catch up – to renew their own capital investment as it were.

Education for leisure overlaps with this other aspect in many ways. Languages are a favourite course in night schools, as are car maintenance and electronics. There are, however, a whole range of subjects which people are interested in and which could be made available on a one day a week, or weekly, quarterly course basis. Some may be frowned upon by the purists as trivial, by others as a waste of time, but ultimately what is wanted is a system which helps people to fulfil their potential and certainly the self-perception of this differs considerably. It is in this sort of area that the expertise of those retired could well be used, as counsellors, for example. This increase in educational demand is job-creating in itself. Not only would teachers and ancillaries be needed, but also the construction and equipment industries would be stimulated.

An emphasis on leisure would suggest that leisure-based industries and technologies would flourish. This would apply especially to information and teaching systems, communications systems and the whole gamut of existing activities from the media and the performing arts, to sport and do-it-yourself. It may well be that a considerable amount of these new developments would be exportable and the favourable effect on the balance of payments should not be underestimated.

White-collar employees have a special interest and special problems associated with this scenario. Their skills are often the ones most liable to premature obsolescence and the retraining/educational programmes are essential, but by and large, unavailable to them even today. Their jobs are often, as we have suggested earlier, the most stressful and in some cases there are no set hours of work. For example, middle and senior management often feel obliged to work twelve- or fifteen-hour days and in some instances contracts merely specify that certain work has to be done. In the managerial areas one attitude to be overcome is the indispensability syndrome. Managers either actually believe, or believe it is in their interests to be seen believing, that if they abandon their post for a moment, their department (if not their ship) would sink. It is a cruel fact of life that almost no one is indispensable – apparently irreparable losses always seem to be repaired quite quickly and smoothly. Managers would be acting in not only their own interests, but probably in the interests of their employers and subordinates too, if they were to avail themselves of possible future changes.

We believe these changes will be well under way before the start of the twenty-first century. They are not intended to be treated as a flippant pseudo-scientifically-based projection. Alongside industrial democracy, the authors believe this is the direction in which the trade unions will move. Furthermore, as the emphasis within trade unions and the labour force itself changes from manual and crafts to white collar and technical, we believe the movement will accelerate. If working for a living can become a part of life rather than its unique aim then the overall quality of life will have improved. One of the sadder aspects of recent government has been the emphasis that the secondary education system is being made to have on 'preparing for work'. Yes, it is important, but must not be allowed to override all the other aspects, because the work might not be there anyway.

Chapter 13

The future

'You cannot fight against the future. Time is on our side.' – Gladstone

There now seems to be a quality of inevitability about the collectivisation of bargaining for every entrant into the labour market. We have seen that there has been unprecedentedly large growth in white-collar trade union membership over the last twenty years and that in the more recent past it has been accelerating.

We have also, in the course of the book, attempted some indication as to the causes of this growth. Some reasons seem central: the labour force has been changing: the manufacturing sector has been shedding labour and within that area there has been a shift to the employment of more white-collar personnel. The service providers and the government sector both increased their demands for labour and these increases were heavily slanted towards the white-collar employees. Technical change has meant the introduction of more capital-intensive processes and the employment of more technicians at the expense of craftsmen. Incomes policies have hit the white-collar worker the hardest, the reorganisation and mergers have added insecurity to the rapidly dwindling, if not actually reversed differentials. Thus we had the pre-conditions for union growth: an expanding catchment area, discontentment amongst employees, and uncertainty as to the future. Add on to this a radically changing social scene with a demand for an industrial suffrage and the impetus for change is overwhelming.

But even all this is not enough as a definitive explanation. White-collar workers not only *needed* to join a union but *wanted* to join.

Few closed shops exist, few agreements were casually conceded by management to stimulate recruitment; indeed, usually the opposite was true: there has been a history of bitter employer resistance. The want came from a new knowledge of what other employees were achieving. In each firm or enterprise, in each profession or skill, there were slightly different factors stimulating union membership. Whether this was the installation of a computer, or a job-evaluation scheme being introduced, poor employee/management communications or, simply, low salaries. The actual reason for joining a union was specific to the enterprise; the other factors becoming a backdrop. The next question is, will this phenomenal rate of growth be sustained?

The composition of the labour force is continuing to change. As a rule-of-thumb, each new investment project is more capital intensive than the last and consequently employs fewer people per £1 invested. Those who are employed tend to need technical skills rather than the traditional trade skills. This is, of course, a generalised view but the onward move to higher technology dictates the long-term trend. Our theory is that the multiplier effects of the new technological investment will stimulate service-sector growth and the consequent increased tax levies stimulate public-sector growth. Both of these sectors employ a high percentage of white-collar staff. Thus, on both counts white-collar employment is likely to rise, and in doing so will increase the catchment area for the unions involved.

In the private sector white-collar union penetration is still well below 50 per cent, so there is great scope for increasing union membership even amongst the existing labour force. In this respect middle-class trade unionism is in its infancy. The Equal Opportunities Act should, in time, provide a stimulus to female membership intake as the career openings emerge and the traditional attitudes change. In the shorter term the continuing incomes policies will erode both in-work differentials and external relativities with respect to manual workers' earnings and so continue to stimulate a steady stream of applicants. In addition, the perceptible moves to shed labour and to increase efficiency and productivity will continue to provide the uncertainty and promote the insecurity that naturally makes employees seek out trade unions.

Those filling many of the new jobs will, of necessity, have to obain technical qualifications and will want an adequate return on this self-investment. Others will be former manual workers who have been retrained and still have a sense of the history and background of trade unionism. Our membership of the EEC should stimulate the insurance and banking industries, thus adding to the pool of white-collar employment. This will all be happening at a time of growing union membership. Within this decade young people will be entering the labour market from backgrounds which already embrace union membership. This is the crucial factor since much of the previous work was to overcome suspicion because the recruiting area was one with a traditionally hostile view of trade unions, this is obviously going to change. The really hard work has now been done; it remains to consolidate and expand.

As technological changes, especially computers and computerised applications, create different work methods they also have a great impact on the structure of the economic and government institutions. On the assumption that the present rate of development will be maintained the movement towards centralisation of decision-making within the larger and larger groupings will also be maintained. Even if both the mini-computer and the silicon chip are used to their full potential, the trend is merely amended, not reversed. One of the major background motivations for white-collar union recruitment has been the creation of the new, large unit with a loss of residual decision-making powers for many administrators and a total alienation for many more. If this trend develops so union membership will increase.

One feature which may become decisive concerns the activity of the multinational company. All unions have problems with this type of enterprise. The difficulties transcend status, national boundaries and politics, for the multinational company owes allegiance to no one except its shareholders (or, probably, its top executives) in the base country. It is neither moved by the economic priorities of countries in which it operates nor does it feel morally bound by the constraints that these may impose. It is in business to make as large a profit as is possible in global terms and if this involves transfer-pricing, bribery or bringing a government down, history has shown that some such companies will not hesitate to do such things.

Negotiating with a multinational is difficult because of the critical lack of sensitive information, which is something that neither the Employment Protection nor Industry Acts will solve. This stems from the fact that a multinational company may not wish to make a profit in a particular country because this might mean making a loss in global terms. Its subsidiaries are often transfer-pricing staging-posts and the lack of profit so useful to the owners in a commercial sense is also used as a stick with which to beat the unions. Details of intra-group trading are essential to combat this. The second point is their mobility and the absolute volume of capital. Investment can be switched from one country to another where there is the incentive of a lower wage system or strong anti-union laws, or even to teach a lesson to a particularly hostile government or militant trade union. Strikes of capital are not unknown, merely unpublished. The size of their operations often mean that the threat of either a withdrawal or the placing of new investment elsewhere is enough to make a government take notice or capitulate.

These factors afflict manual and white-collar unions and governments alike and although governments can act, few do. Most countries have some foreign investment monitoring, but Britain seems exceptional in not wishing to attempt this. Trade unions, on the other hand, must take up the challenge, try and deal with the problem and work to an international basis.

The trend to concentration will have to be mirrored in the trade union movement itself. This will not only be as a result of technology virtually removing many of the old trades and industries on which the present membership is based, although this will play a considerable part. Smaller unions will not be able to afford the services needed to represent their membership adequately. The legal, research, health and safety, pensions and job-evaluation functions are all costly and a union has to be able to finance these activities. It can do it by having experts on the staff or it can buy from outside on a fee-per-item basis. The important thing is that it must be done.

The economies of scale that a large grouping can give are of considerable importance. As we approach the era of the expansion of collective bargaining into planning agreements, corporate plans and industrial democracy, so the need for a fully-trained and expert staff, both negotiating and back-up will become even more apparent. By the late 1980s it is unlikely that there will be more than fifty TUC affiliates. It is also likely that, by this point, there will be at least one, very large private-sector based general white-collar union. This will be moving towards a million members and will be a pace-setter for all white-collar employees. There will also be less than fifteen TUC-affiliated unions catering exclusively for white-collar employees at this point. Not unnaturally such changes, if they happen, will have profound effects on the TUC itself.

Along with the entire trade union movement the unions of salaried staffs will have to cope with technological changes, changes in bargaining itself, changes in government and changes in the *mores* of society. Of all the unions, those in the white-collar sector, which have been forced to use the most professional techniques by their membership, will be the most flexible and the most easily adaptable. These techniques will have to become more sophisticated themselves. The quality and depth of the professional officials will have to increase and the back-up services will have to expand, both qualitatively and quantitatively.

The new freedoms and rights which are now being demanded by the movement as a whole will bring with them responsibilities and the white-collar unions and their members will not shirk them. To take advantage of these rights, however, will require modified attitudes and a far deeper knowledge of how government and industry actually work. Unions will have to train members to be experts in pensions, in health and safety, and in business economics because instead of one group representative or steward there will be specialist representatives. It will be a new trade unionism to match the new circumstances. It will not necessarily be less militant or less dependent on its collective base, it will be based on the model of the existing white-collar unions to the extent that officer coverage, communications and back-up are permanent. Professionalism plus commitment is always superior to commitment alone, and the professional trade union movement's day is just dawning.

The white-collar unions have grown in response to needs. These needs will increase in both industrial and job-status terms over time. The legislation package so recently introduced will, if used properly, soberly and imaginatively be of benefit to their entire membership. By the year 2000 the notion that there were employees who, for status reasons, eschewed trade unions, will be laughable. By then the emphasis of the trade unions will probably have changed from instant reaction to events to one of medium-term planning. But the essence, the solidarity and the collectivity will still remain the vital impellers. As we all adjust to collectivity, the yeast in the social dough will be the addition of the salariat to the most representative trade union movement in the world.

Index

academic investigations, 31-3
ACAS, 57, 93, 97-100, 102, 124
Acts, *see* Employment Protection;
    Equal Pay; Grants, Charges etc.;
    Health and Safety; Industrial
    Relations; Industry; Sex Dis-
    crimination; Shops, Offices etc.;
    Social Security; Trades Union,
    etc.
ACTSS, 31, 43, 81
administration, 18, 46
advertising: and expectations, 113,
    142; job, 103; and unions, 55-6;
    unisex, 105
AESD, 29
affiliations: to Labour Party, 69,
    79-81; to TUC, 4-7, 41-2, 69,
    81
agriculture, 4, 16, 151-2
alienation, 108, 127-8, 149
APEX: bargaining, 98; finance, 59;
    and government, 80; and inform-
    ation, 103; journals, 63; and law,
    81; membership, 31, 32, 35, 36,
    42, 45-6, 57; officials, 67; recruit-
    ment, 72; research in, 64; and
    strikes, 74, 78
appraisal, 90-1
APST, 47
arbitration, 65, 92-3; *see also* ACAS
artists' union, *see* SLADE
ASSET, 29-30, 33-4
ASTMS: bargaining, 98; education in,
    61; finance, 59, 93; and govern-
    ment, 80, 82, 116-17, 137; and
    information, 103; and law, 64,

81; membership, 9, 29-36, 42,
    45-51, 56, 138; officials, 67, 100;
    and pay, 138; on pensions, 135;
    and publicity, 54; and quasi-
    unions, 50, 52; and recruitment,
    53, 55, 59, 94, 148; research in,
    64; and safety, 108; and strikes,
    74, 77
AUEW, 30, 43, 81

Bain, George, 33-4, 36
balance of payments, 125
banking: employees, 18-19, 26;
    unions in, 30, 45-6; *see also*
    NUBE
bargaining, collective, 122; ASTMS,
    98; extension of, 126, 130-1,
    163; formalities of, 71; and ICI,
    82; non-union, 51; NUBE, 52-3;
    for pensions, 121; productivity,
    91-2; small union, 52; time off
    for, 100
BIM, 141, 144-5
'black jacket' workers, 43
blacklisting, 119-20
BMA, 47, 50-2; *see also* health
    services
bonuses, 84, 91
Budgets, 83, 89, 116, 119
Bullock Report, 96, 130, 134, 142

CAC, 93, 97, 103
catch-up process, 123
CAWU, 29-30
CBI, 102, 134, 144-5
CEI, 52

Census, 14, 16, 140, 146
certification of unions, 41-2, 49-50,
97-8, 138, 148; *see also* recognition
CFDT, 124
CGT, 124
change: commitment to, 96; in
industrial relations, 124-35; in
labour, 9, 37; *see also* computers;
education; growth; technology
CIR, 81-2, 98
Civil Service unions, 7, 25-32, 42-6,
51, 82-4, 148; *see also* CPSA;
IPCS; SCS
class, 136; *see also* status
clerks' unions, 27-30, 46-7; *see also*
ACTSS; APEX; CAWU; TGWU
closed shop, 163
closure, company, 85, 101
COHSE, 30, 35, 43, 51; *see also* health
services
communication in unions, 63
companies, types of, 131-2
computers: and employment, 15;
in industry, 54, 56, 142, 154,
157, 164; operators, *see* APEX;
in unions, 62
concentration of industry, 127, 149,
165-6
concessions, 89; *see also* salary package
conciliation, 97-8; *see also* ACAS
Confederation of Employee Organisations, 51
Conservative Party, 116-17, 137,
145; *see also* parliament
construction industry, *see* UCATT
cost-cutting, 84
Counter-Inflation policy, 92
CPSA: journals, 63; membership,
32, 35, 36, 46, 57, 138; officials,
67; and politics, 137; research in,
75; strikes, 75
Cripps, Sir Stafford, 7, 113

damages, legal, 99
danger, *see* safety
DATA, 73
decrease in union membership, 35
democracy, industrial, 126-35
Denmark, unions, 126
DHSS, 51; *see also* health services;
social security

differentials, pay, 44, 53, 83, 141-4;
see also earnings
Directors, Institute of, 108
discrimination, 104; *see also* women
dismissal, 72, 74, 98
dispute-pay, 77-8
disputes, *see* strikes
dissatisfaction, *see* alienation
distribution of white-collar workers,
17-18
Donovan Commission, 33
draughtsmen's unions, 29-30, 46; *see
also* AESD; DATA; TASS

earnings, 20-1, 38, 44, 75-8, 84; *see
also* differentials; equal pay;
income; salary package
Earnings Survey, New (1977), 14-17
39
economy, *see* industry
education: changes in, 160-1; discrimination in, 104; employment
in, 19; loss of security in, 84;
strikes in, 75; in unions, 60-1, 99-
101, 137; unions in, 26, 28, 31,
46, 133; and work, 153; *see also*
NAS/UWT; NUET; NUT
EEC, 125-6, 129, 131, 142, 164
EEF, 33, 75
EEPTU, 4, 43
efficiency, 129
Election, General, 23
electricity industry, 30, 115; *see also*
AEI: EEPTU: EPEA
elitism, 48
EMA, 48
employee, *see* worker
employment: agencies, 82; and computer, 15; high, 17-18; pattern, 9
Employment Appeal Tribunal, 50
Employment Medical Advisory
Service, 108
Employment Protection Act (1975),
3, 96; and certification, 41, 47,
49; and information, 109; and
intimidation, 72-3; and management, 142, 165; and maternity
leave, 89, 103; and redundancy,
84; and secondment, 61; and
union membership, 93, 97-8
engineers' unions, 46, 48, 52, 75-6;
see also AESD; AUEW; EEF;
TASS; UKAPE

entertainment unions, 45; *see also* media; musicians; theatre
EPEA, 48
Equal Opportunities Commission, 105
equal pay, 83
Equal Pay Act, 56, 78
evaluation, *see* job
expansion, union, *see* growth
expectations, 113, 142, 153
expenditure, public, 8

failure, company, 85, 101
family companies, 132, 156-7
Fifth Directive, 125-6, 142
finance, union, 59-61, 93
First Division Association, 31
flexitime, 89-90
Force ouvrière, 124
forces, armed, 4
foremen's unions, 29, 46; *see also* ASSET
France: paternity leave, 160; unions, in, 101, 124, 127
Friendly Societies, 26, 33-4, 59
F&SMBS, 33-4

G&MWU, 88
Germany, West: industry, 19-20, 124, 132; unions, 126
government, central, *see* parliament
government, local, unions in, 7, 18, 27, 29, 46, 75, 84
Grants, Charges and Remuneration Act, 118-19
grouping: of industries, 166; of unions, 44-6
growth of unions, 1-7, 45, 122-3, 148, 167; *see also* membership
Grunwick dispute, 72, 74, 98-9

health at work, 106-8, 156
health services: employment in, 19-20; non-unions in, 51; unions in, 30, 47; *see also* BMA; COHSE; MPU; NHS
Health and Safety Act (1974), 96, 106
hierarchies, management, 142-3
holding companies, 132
holidays, 84, 87, 150, 156
Holland, unions, 126
hostility to management, 147
hours of work, 84, 89, 155-9; *see also* shifts

ICI and unions, 81-2, 131-2
Inbucon Survey, 144
incentives, 145; *see also* salary package
income, *see* earnings
incomes policies, 39, 54, 82, 84, 112-23, 138, 144, 149
increments, 91, 121-2, 138
independence, *see* certification
indispensability syndrome, 161
Industrial Relations Act (1970), 23
Industrial Relations Act (1971), 3, 7; Commission on, 50, 97; and dismissal, 98; and law, 81, 100; and quasi-unions, 73; registration under, 41, 47; repealed, 82, 96; and unions, 93, 95, 117, 125
industrial relations and white-collar unions, 124-35, 138-9
Industrial Revolution, 24-5
industry: computers in, 54, 56, 142, 154, 157, 164; democracy in, 126-35; development of, 4, 24-5; foreign, 19-20, 101, 124, 126, 132, 148; heavy, white-collar unions in, 26-7, 29, 34-5, 45-6, 148; importance, 16; nationalised, 7, 29-30, 42, 148-9
Industry Act (1975), 3, 96, 108, 142, 165
inflation, 39, 54, 112, 119, 123
information in unions, 101-3, 109, 133, 149
Inland Revenue, *see* IRS; tax
insecurity and union membership, 37-9; *see also* security
insurance: employees, 18-19; unions in, 27, 29, 35, 46, 98, 119; *see also* NUIW; UIS
International Labour Office, 155
intimidation, 72-3
investment, 20, 129, 154, 159
IPCS, 7, 30-1, 63
IRSF, 57

Japan, 19
job: advertisement, 103; content, 13; evaluation, 38, 61-2, 78-9; image, 142; ranking, 14-15, 113; security, 84-5, 142, 146; titles, 15-16, 21
journalists' unions, 45, 75
journals, union, 62-3

labour force, 9, 31-2, 37, 113, 154, 164

Labour Party: and incomes, 115–16, 118–20; and productivity bargaining, 91–2; and unions, 125; *see also* affiliation; parliament
law and unions, 64, 81, 95–111; *see also* Acts
legislation, *see* Acts; law
leisure, 156–7, 160–1
life, quality of, 151–62
local government unions, *see* government
London, 17–18

management, 108, 126, 134, 140–50; *see also* BIM; EMA; MATSA; staff associations
Management Centre, 143
manpower projection, 40
manual occupations, 14–17, 39
market research, 18
maternity leave, 89, 103–4
MATSA, 42–4
media, 23, 54–6, 146; *see also* advertising
medicine, *see* health services
membership, union, 9, 29–36, 42–53, 56–7, 62–3, 138–9; *see also* decrease; growth; recruitment
mergers: industrial, 30, 37–8, 149; union, 47, 56
merit-awards, 91
Midlands, 17
militancy, 76
miners, *see* NUM; strikes
mobility, 46, 58–9
MPU, 47, 51; *see also* health services
multi-companies, 131–2
multinational companies, 30, 37, 69, 110–11, 131–2, 165
musicians, 13; unions, 27–8; *see also* entertainment

NALGO: education in, 62; finance of, 59; and government, 80; journals, 63; and law, 64; membership, 32, 36, 42, 45–6, 63, 139; officials, 67; and pay negotiations, 138; research in 64; in TUC, 7, 31, 35
NAS/UWT, 32
National Enterprise Board, 85
nationalisation, *see* industry
NEDC, 139

NEDO, 8, 82
negotiation, 58, 66–8, 138; *see also* bargaining; earnings
newspapers, *see* media
NFA, 29
NFPW, 28
NHS: origins, 29; unions in, 30, 42–5, 51–2, 55, 80; *see also* health services
NIESR, 123
non-manual occupations, 14–17, 20, 30, 37, 39
non-union unions, 50–1; *see also* quasi-unions
North England, 17
NUBE: arbitration, 63; and information, 103; journals, 63; and law, 81; membership, 30–2, 35, 36, 45–6, 53; officials, 67; and quasi-unions, 50, 52–3; and recognition, 73
NUGMW, 30, 43
NUIW, 35, 36
NUM, 35, 36
NUPE, 30, 35, 43, 51, 138
nursing, 20, 82, 84; *see also* health services
Nursing, Royal College of, 51
NUS, 94
NUT: development, 7, 26, 35; education in, 62; legal department, 64; journals, 63; membership, 32, 57, 138; officials, 67; research in, 64

officials, union, 66-70, 100; training, 67
overtime, 22, 87

paperwork, union, 62–3
parliament and unions, 33–4, 50, 79–82; 116–17, 137; *see also* Labour Party
Parsons, C.A., 73
part-time work, 4
participation, *see* worker-directors
paternity leave, 160
pay, *see* earnings
Pay Board, 117
pensions, 84, 87–8, 106, 121, 134–5, 138, 158
PIB, 115
planning agreements, 109–10, 123

police, 4, 7
politics, *see* parliament
post office unions, 26–8, 30, 32, 45,
    107
prevention of unionisation, 33–4, 149
Price Commission, 117-18
Prices and Incomes Bill, 115–16
Prices and Incomes Board, 33
prison officers' unions, 28
private sector unions, 35, 41–2, 67,
    75–6, 147–9, 164
production line, managerial, 142
productivity, 91–2, 157–8
Professional and Executive Register,
    144, 146
profile, high and low, 76–7
projection, labour, 31–2
promotion, 43, 46, 145
Protestant ethic, 151–3
public sector unions, 41–2, 69,
    75–6, 82, 147–9; *see also* CPSA;
    NUPE
publicity, 54

quasi-unions, 47–8, 50–1, 52–3, 73

radio, *see* media
railway unions, 26–30, 35, 45, 148;
    see also NUR; TSSA
ranking, *see* job
recognition, union, 33, 71–5, 82,
    97–9; *see also* certification
recruitment, union, 22–3, 28, 53–9,
    72–3, 93–4, 148; *see also* member-
    ship
redundancy, 53, 84–5, 101
Referendum, 95
registration, *see* certification
reinstatement, 99
representation, 66–7, 71–2
research, union, 64–5, 101
restraint, wage, *see* incomes policies
retirement, 157–9
rewards, 86–94
role of unions, 8

Sabbaticals, 160
safety, 96, 106–9
salary package, 83–4, 87–94, 105,
    143–4, 150; *see also* earnings
salary surveys, 65
sanctions, government, 119–20
scientists' unions, *see* APST; ASTMS

Scottish Trades Union Congress, 42
SCS, 7, 32, 137–8
security, job, 84–5, 142, 146
self-employed, 4
service industries, 19
Sex Discrimination Act, 17, 36, 96,
    103–5; *see also* women
share-holding, 93
shifts, 87, 155–9; *see also* hours
shipbuilding unions, *see* AESD
shop assistants' union, 27, 30, 46;
    see also COHSE
Shops, Offices and Railways Premises
    Act, 90
single-industry unions, 45
SLADE, 55–6
slump, 146
Social Contract, 96, 118
social security, 29, 58
Social Security Pensions Act (1978),
    96, 106
South England, 17–18
special register, 47; *see also* quasi-
    unions
specialisation, 153
staff associations, 47–50, 73, 81,
    148–9
'staff' concept, 13
'stagflation', 123
status, white-collar: and earnings,
    20–1, 38, 44, 84; removal of, 84;
    and self-perception, 10, 44, 136;
    and unions, 43; and work environ-
    ment, 25, 90, 147; *see also* class
stress, 108, 156, 158–9
Strife, In Place of, 116
strikes: air traffic control, 121; of
    capital, 165; in education, 75;
    General, 29; and income loss, 64;
    increase in, 75–7; Miners', 23, 76,
    117; and quasi-unions, 73; reasons
    for, 77–8, 82; and recognition,
    73–5; and recruitment, 72; rotat-
    ing, 77; and social security, 58;
    and staff associations, 73, 81; *see
    also* individual unions
structure, union, 62–6
students' union, *see* NUS
subscriptions, *see* finance
Sudreau Report, 127, 154
supervisors' union, *see* ASSET
Sweden: paternity leave, 160; unions,
    101, 124, 126, 132, 148

take-overs, 54, 111; *see also* mergers
.TASS: finance of, 59; journals, 63;
  and law, 81; membership, 31, 32,
  35, 36, 42, 45–6, 48, 50, 62;
  officials, 67; and politics, 80, 137;
  and quasi-unions, 50; research in,
  64–5; strikes, 73
Tavistock Attitude Survey, 81
tax, 83, 89, 101, 119, 143–6
teachers, *see* education
technologists' union, *see* APST
technology, change in, 2-5, 9, 164;
  see also computers; industry
television, *see* media
T&GWU, 30–1, 43, 47, 88, 102
theatre unions, 27
time off, right to, 100
titles, job, 15–16, 21
Trades Union and Labour Relations
  Act (1974), 41, 51, 96, 98
transport unions, 45, 75, 149; *see
  also* railways; T&GWU; TSSA
travel to work, 156, 158–9
tribunals, industrial, 99
TSSA: communications in, 63;
  finance, 59; and government,
  80; journals, 63; membership,
  30, 35, 36, 44–5, 148; officials, 67
TUC: affiliation with, 4–7, 41–2, 69,
  81, 147–8, 166; education in,
  60–1; and incomes policies, 112–
  23, 138; and independent affiliates,
  47–51; membership, 24–42; and
  retirement, 158; and unemployment, 28
turnover, union, 58–9

UCATT, 43
uncertainty, *see* insecurity

unemployment, 28, 38, 84, 112, 146,
  153–5, 160
UIS, 30
UKAPE, 47
UNESCO, 10
unionisation: of management, 143;
  prevention of, 33–4, 149; *see also*
  membership
United States, 19, 74, 108, 124
USDAW, 30, 35, 55, 138

victimisation, 72–3, 105
vouchers, 89

wages, *see* earnings
Wales Trade Union Council, 42
warehousemen's unions, 27
Wars, World, 7, 27, 29
Welfare State, *see* social security
white-collar workers: defined, 10–15,
  37; distribution of, 17–18; growth
  of, 9–11, 18–20, 35–8; *see also*
  membership; status
Whitley, J.H., 29
Wilson, Sir Harold, 135
women: employment of, 16–18, 28;
  and flexitime, 90; and job advertisements, 105; pay, 77–9, 83,
  105–6; promotion, 103; in unions,
  54, 57, 67, 100; *see also* maternity
  leave; Sex Discrimination
work: and education, 153; opportunities, 154–5; sanctity of, 151–
  3; structure, 126–7; *see also* job;
  labour
worker-directors, 127–35, 142
worker-trustees, 134
workers, concept of, 13
workplace conditions, 25, 90, 147;
  see also safety